Provided

by

Measure B

which was approved

by the voters in

November, 1998

WindowDressing

From the Editors of Vogue & Butterick

B

The Butterick Publishing Company
161 Sixth Ave
New York, NY 10013

Contents

Chapter 1   Basics

Chapter 2   Valances

Chapter 3   Drapes

Chapter 4   Reversibles

Chapter 5   Panels

Chapter 6 Window Drapery

Introduction & Acknowledgements

When Ebeneezer Butterick founded Butterick Patterns in 1863, he revolutionized the home sewing industry by creating multi-sized paper patterns for clothing. When looking to write this book, we realized that, unlike clothing, window dressings do not always need to follow a paper pattern. We looked through our Vogue and Butterick catalogs, containing hundreds of styles and selected twenty-five of our best window treatment designs. That's the equivalent of ten different pattern envelopes in one easy - to - understand book!

You will find window dressings to suit any room or decor, from quick and easy panels, curtains and valances to elaborate and elegant window drapery. We'll show you not just how to dress a window, but how to do it in style.

In revising these patterns, we relied on the help of many different people. We would like to thank Susanna Stratton-Norris, DeBare Saunders and Mario Buatta for the use of their lovely designs, and of all our production staff below.

Editor: Caroline Politi
Technical Editor: Deborah Woodbridge
Associate Managing Editors: Stephanie Marracco and Nicole Pressly
Copy Editor: Beth Baumgartel
Illustrations: Debra Panteleo and Elizabeth Berry
Photography: Brian Kraus, Juan Rios, unidentified photographer for Chapter 6
Licensing Director: Joe Anselmo
Page Builder: David Joinnides
Indexer: Nan Badgett
Design: Triad Design Group, Ltd.
President: Art Joinnides

Manufactured in the United States of America

10 9 8 7 6 5 4 3 2 1

Library of Congress Card Catalog Number: 97-077519

ISBN 1-57389-015-4

First Edition

The Butterick Publishing Company
161 Sixth Ave
New York, NY 10013

Measuring Your Window

There are many elements to consider when decorating your home. A window dressing is wonderfully versatile, and surprisingly easy to make. Whatever your décor, you can create a beautiful window treatment for your decorating scheme.

More than mere decoration, window dressings also serve a function. They filter sunlight, add privacy, or block a chilly winter draft. Consider both form and function, to devise unique solutions for all your decorating demands. Your creativity is the only limit!

Once you select a style, the next step is measuring your window. Here is a diagram that shows all the measurements that you may need to take. Be sure to take the measurements that are relevant for the style you have chosen. For example, if you are planning to make a shade, you need the inside molding measurement, from side to side, and from top to sill.

In order to calculate your fabric yardage, you need to compare your window measurements with those given in the instructions for the design you wish to make. Most of the projects in this book are suitable for windows 36" (91.5 cm) to 42" (107 cm) wide. If the window you are dressing is a different length or width from the window in the instructions, you need to add or subtract from the yardage stated in the materials list. Read through the cutting instructions first; knowing how the fabric is cut is key to figuring your yardage.

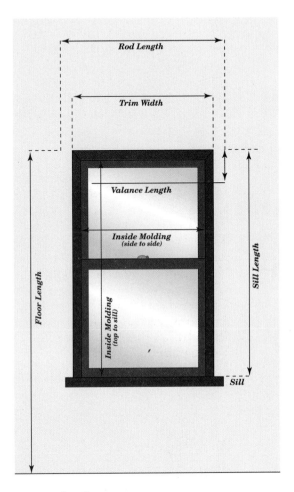

For a difference in *length,* you need to know if the window dressing is made of multiple widths of fabric. Simply multiply the number of fabric widths times the difference in window lengths to determine the difference in yardage. For instance, if your window is 36" (91.5 cm) longer than the pattern in the book, and the pattern asks for two pieces of fabric, each the full width, multiply 36 (91.5 cm) by two. In this example you need an additional 72" (1.83 m) to complete the project.

For a difference in *width*, you need to know the width of the pieces of fabric required. For a window dressing that is not pleated or gathered, you only need enough additional fabric to account for the difference between your window and the one given in the instruction. For a pleated style, you need to decide how many more pleats should be added (or subtracted, if your window is smaller) to achieve the desired look. The difference in width between the windows, plus the amount required for extra pleats, is your extra yardage calculation. For gathered styles, note the ratio of fullness — usually, it is 2:1. This helps you figure out if you need more or less to complete the project.

Rods and Hardware

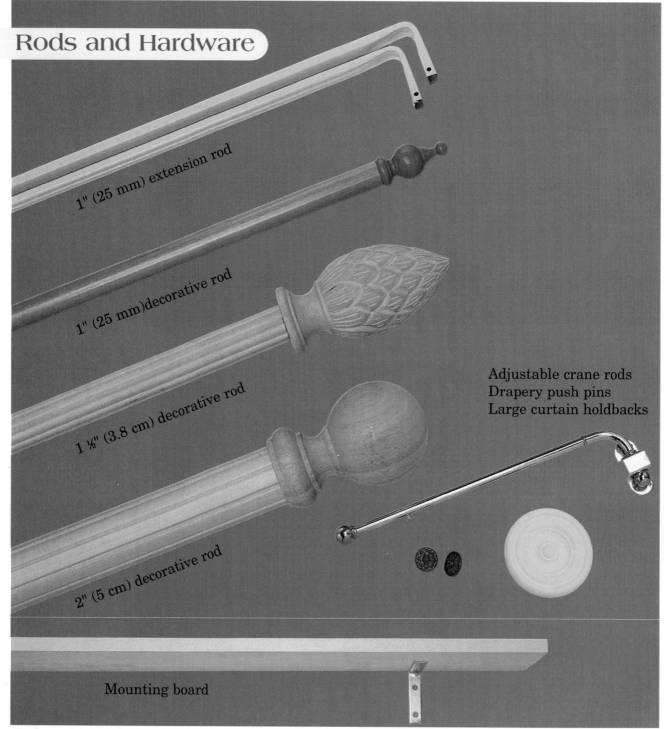

1" (25 mm) extension rod

1" (25 mm) decorative rod

1 ½" (3.8 cm) decorative rod

2" (5 cm) decorative rod

Adjustable crane rods
Drapery push pins
Large curtain holdbacks

Mounting board

Rods and hardware are very important components in planning your window dressing. The rod or hardware you choose could be a subtle support, a dramatic accent, or a contrast of style or color. You can easily purchase a wide variety of these pieces, or custom-create them yourself. For example, make your own rod by attaching an object to each end of a wooden dowel — building blocks for baby's room-seashells, wooden beads, or whatever else strikes your fancy.

In the materials list for each project, we list the type and size of rod and/or hardware needed. Here we show a sampling of the type of items you may need.

sewing information

In general, ½" (13 mm) seam allowances are included in the measurements given in all cutting instructions. If a particular seam requires a different seam allowance, it is mentioned at that time.

Press as you sew. For most seams, particularly straight seams, press flat, then press open. This gives a smooth, professional appearance to your work. Some seams may

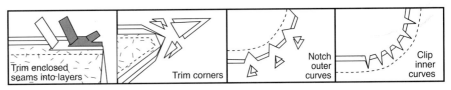

Trim enclosed seams into layers   Trim corners   Notch outer curves   Clip inner curves

not require this method of pressing, such as, those that join decorative fabric and lining. In this case, the work must be turned first and then pressed. In the instructions for each style, directions for pressing are given. Clip seam allowance at inner corners and curves, so they lie flat.

Glossary

Bias: Diagonal direction; 45˚ from the lengthwise grain and crosswise grain. See page 95.

Easestitch: Using a machine stitch of approximately six to eight stitches per inch (2.5 cm), stitch ½" (13 mm) from the edge mentioned in sewing instructions, leaving 6" (15 cm) thread ends at each end of stitching. Do not back stitch at either end. Pull thread ends adjust fit.

Edgestitch: This stitch is used to give a nice crisp edge to a hem or to secure an edge in place. This stitch is also used as a design feature, with or without topstitching. Using a regular stitch, stitch close to a seam or finished edge.

Gather: This stitch is used to treat an area that needs to be gathered. Using a machine stitch of approximately six to eight stitches per inch (25 mm), stitch ½" (13 mm) from the edge and again ¼" (6 mm) from edge, leaving 6"

(15 cm) thread ends at each end of stitching. Pull thread ends to adjust gathers to fit.

Grain: Lengthwise grain: fabric threads running parallel to the selvage. *Crosswise grain:* fabric threads running perpendicular to the lengthwise grain and selvage.

Interfacing: A fabric used to give a window treatment body and opacity. It is sandwiched between the decorative and lining fabrics.

Narrow hem: Useful for hemming sheer fabrics. Turn in ½" (13 mm); press, easing fullness, if necessary. Open out hem. Turn in again so raw edge is along pressed crease; press. Turn in along first crease; stitch.

Selvage: The tightly woven finished lengthwise edges of fabric, usually about ¼" (6 mm) to ½" (13 mm) wide. It is along the selvage that fabric manufacturers might features color

keys of the colors used in the printing of the fabric's design and/or repeat indicator.

Slipstitch: A very useful stitch, most commonly used for closing an opening that was used for turning. Slide your needle through one folded edge for approximately ¼" (6 mm), then through the opposite folded edge, drawing thread so that the two edges meet. To hem, slide your needle through the inner folded edge of the hem approximately ¼" (6 mm) and then pick up a thread or two from the fabric behind the hem.

Topstitch: A decorative or functional stitch. Using desired machine stitch length, stitch ¼" (6 mm) from the edge or seam, using your presser foot as a guide if possible. (Most sewing machines measure ¼" (6 mm) from the needle position to the side edge of the presser foot, so it makes a handy guide.)

Valances

are the most versatile of all the window dressings. They range from a simple band hung from a mounting board or continental rod, to a complex combination of swags and jabots. And since you are using minimal yardage, you can choose that wild, or expensive, fabric that you wouldn't use on a larger project. Their size also makes them ideal for smaller spaces. And what better way to hide the unsightly brackets of blinds or shades? Embellish valances with elaborate trims, hang them from decorative rods, or match them with any manner of drapes, and the possibilities are endless.

Pointed Valance combines simplicity with elegance, making it perfect for the window that requires a light touch. You can customize this valance in a number of ways. Instead of tassels, hang threaded beads, or miniature toys for a child's room.

materials list

- ◆ 3½" tassels — 9 for a 36" (91.5 cm) window, 11 for a 42" (107 cm) window
- ◆ 5⅜ yds. (5 m) of ⅝" (15 mm) grosgrain ribbon
- ◆ Two angle irons and hardware
- ◆ Carpet tacks
- ◆ Hammer
- ◆ 1" x 4" (2.5 cm x 10 cm) mounting board, cut the same length as window width, painted if desired.

Fabric Suggestions:
Medium weight fabrics, such as polished cotton, chintz, and damask.

- ◆ 1⅜ yds. (1.25 m) fabric, 45" (115 cm) to 60" (152 cm) wide
- ◆ 1⅜ yds. (1.25 m) contrast lining, 45" (115 cm) to 60" (152 cm) wide

36" or a 42" wide window

cutting instructions

1
36" (91.5 cm) Window:
For the center, cut one section 41" (104 cm) wide and 21" (53.5 cm) long.
For the sides, cut two sections, each 17" (43 cm) wide and 21" (53.5 cm) long.

2
42" (107 cm) Window:
For the center, cut one section 41" (104 cm) wide and 21" (53.5 cm) long.
For the sides, cut two sections, each 23" (58.5 cm) wide and 21" (53.5 cm) long.

3
Stitch the side sections to the center section at each side. To shape lower edge of valance, refer to template and instructions on page 94. Prepare the contrast lining in the same manner.

tips

Not only are the points at the hem of this valance a terrific touch for the window, they add charm to a mantel cover at Christmas time or a tablecloth for any special occasion.

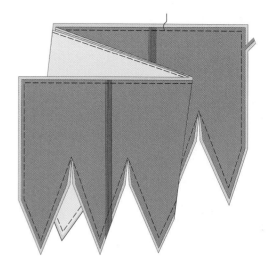

1 With right sides together, pin the valance and contrast lining together. Stitch along outer edges, pivoting at the corners, and leaving an opening at the upper edge for turning. Clip to the pivot points at inside corners, as shown. Trim points.

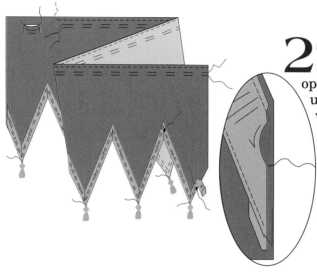

2 Turn the valance right side out, fully turning all outer edges and corners. Press. Slipstitch the opening at the upper edge closed. Edgestitch the upper edge of the valance. Gather upper edge with large machine stitches, ¾" (2 cm) and 1" (2.5 cm) from the finished edge. Pin grosgrain ribbon to the lower edges, folding in fullness at corners and turning in ½" (13 mm) on ends at side edges, as shown. Stitch close to both long edges of the ribbon. Slipstitch ribbon ends and corners. Sew tassels to the points.

3 Position the mounting board above the upper edge of the window frame and mark the position of the angle irons on the wall and mounting boards. Install the angle irons on the board, following the manufacturer's instructions. Mark the center of the mounting board at the front edge.

4 Fold the valance in half; pin mark the center at the upper edge. Lap the valance 1¾" (4.5 cm) over upper edge of mounting board. Tack at the sides and at the center. Adjust the gathers evenly along the mounting board. Tack the remaining edge of the valance in place. Trim the thread ends. Install the finished valance at markings.

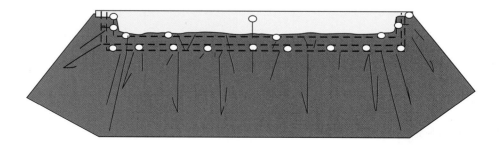

his valance allows a lot of light in, giving the window an open airy look. The strong curves of the spearpoint present a magnificent appearance, while the trim adds a touch of delicacy. In this photo, the valance is made of a dark, luxurious tapestry fabric, giving it a grand style. But if it were made from a light toned floral print, it would have a more whimsical look.

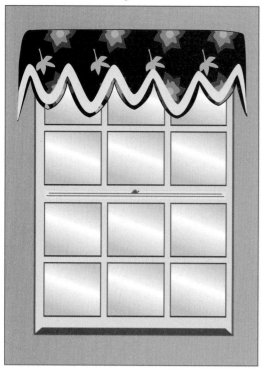

36" and 42" wide window

materials list

Fabric Suggestions:
Almost any weight tapestry fabric, home decorating fabric, cotton broadcloth or silk dupioni.

◆ 1⅛ yds. (1.1 m) fabric, 45" (115 cm) or 60" (152 cm) wide for 36" (91.5 cm) window; 60" (152 cm) wide for 42" (107 cm) window.

◆ Heavy weight non-fusible interfacing, the same measurement as above.

◆ 3 yds. (2.75 m) 1½" (3.8 cm) decorative trim

◆ Two angle irons and hardware

◆ Carpet tacks

◆ Hammer

◆ 1" x 6" (2.5 cm x 15 cm) mounting board, the same length as window width. Painted, if desired.

cutting instructions

1 36" (91.5 cm) Window:
For the valance and lining, cut two sections of fabric, each 43" (109 cm) wide and 19" (48 cm) long. Prepare the interfacing in same manner.

2 42" (107 cm) Window:
For the valance and lining, cut two sections of fabric, each 49" (125 cm) wide and 19" (48 cm) long. Prepare the interfacing in same manner.

3 To shape lower edge of valance, valance lining and mounting board, refer to templates and instructions on page 94.

tips

The points at the hem of this valance add an elegant touch to drapes - perfect for that set of drapes that hang over a radiator or piece of furniture, that don't go to the floor, but need a bit of polish.

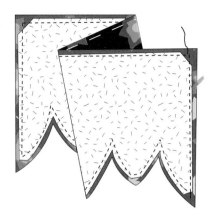

1 Pin the interfacing to wrong side of the valance. Trim corners, as shown. Baste a scant ½" (13 mm) from all the edges. Trim interfacing close to the basting.

2 Pin the decorative trim to the interfaced valance, having the lower edge of the trim ¾" (20 mm) from the valance lower edge, easing in any fullness at the corners and having raw edges even at the side edges. Stitch close to both long edges of the trim.

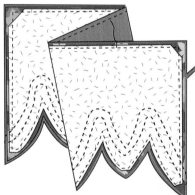

3 With right sides together, pin the valance and the valance lining together. Stitch, pivoting at all corners, leaving an opening for turning at the upper edge. Trim. Clip to the inner corners, as shown.

4 Turn the valance right side out, fully turning all outer edges and corners. Press. Slipstitch the opening at the upper edge. Edgestitch the upper edge of the valance.

5 Position the mounting board above the window, as desired, marking the position for the angle irons on the wall and mounting board. Install the angle irons on the mounting board. Fold the valance in half; pin marking center at the upper edge. Lap the valance 1½" (3.8 cm) over the upper edge of the mounting board. Tack the valance to the board at ends and at center. Tack the remaining edge of the valance in place, easing in fullness around the curves, as shown.
Install the valance at the markings.

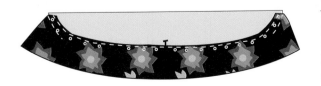

Cord and Tassel Valance

ransform a simple valance into an elegant window dressing! The cord and tassels add substance to the billowing fabric, and provide an extra decorating element. When made from brocade trimmed with silken cord, this treatment looks regal and sophisticated, however when made in a lighthearted print and cotton cords, this same valance has a casual feel.

materials list

◆ 3 yds. (2.75 m) fabric, 45" (115 cm) to 60" (152 cm) wide for 42" (107 cm) window

◆ 8½ yds. (7.75 m) of a ½" (1.3 cm) cord

◆ 8 tassels

◆ 1" (2.5 cm) extension rod with 3" (7.5 cm) return

Fabric Suggestions: Cotton voile, silk chiffon, light weight brocade or cotton gingham do an equally nice job.

◆ 2 yds. (1.83 m) fabric, 45"(115 cm) to 60" (152 cm) wide for 36" (91.5 cm) window

36" or a 42" wide window

cutting instructions

1 36" (91.5 cm) Window:
Cut two sections, each the width of fabric and 31" (79 cm) long.

2 42" (107 cm) Window:
Cut three sections, each the width of fabric and 31" (79 cm) long.

tips

Another pretty look is achieved by using silk garlands of greenery instead of the cord and clusters of flowers instead of the tassels.

Or, for exotic appeal, string beads in place of cord and use beaded tassels to finish the design. Venetian glass beads would look terrific on a valance of silk chiffon.

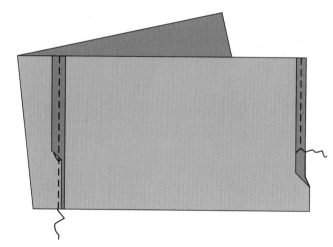

1 With right sides together, stitch the side edges of the valance sections together, leaving the outermost edges free.
Make a narrow hem at the inside edges of the valance.

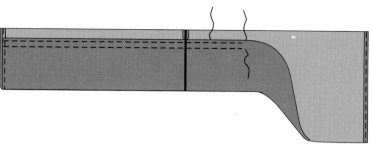

2 To hem the valance, turn up 14" (36 cm) from the lower edge; press. Baste upper edge of hem in place. Stitch ½"(13 mm) and 1½" (4 cm) from the upper raw edge.

3 For the casing, turn down 2" (5 cm) from the upper edge, turning in ½" (13 mm) on the raw edge; press. Slipstitch the pressed edge over the upper stitching.

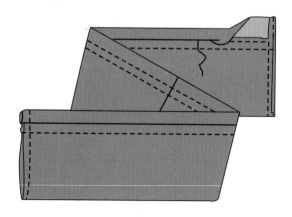

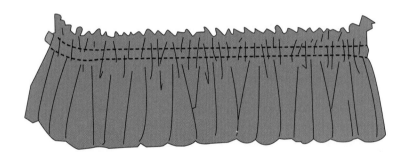

4 Insert the rod into the valance casing; adjusting the valance evenly along the rod.

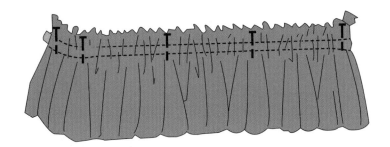

5 Measure 2" (5 cm) from each end of the rod; mark. Divide the distance between the markings into three equal sections; mark. Add pins at both ends.

6 Cut one piece of cord the length of rod, plus 34" (87 cm).
Starting 3" (7.5 cm) from one end of the cord, make a loose knot and pin it in place at the first marking. Make loose knots at remaining rod markings; pin them in place.

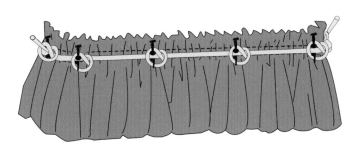

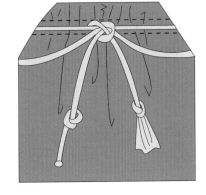

7 For swags, cut five pieces of cord, each 27" (69 cm) long. Starting at the left side, slide one swag through first knot into next knot, having one end even and the remaining end extending approximately 18" (46 cm), as shown.
Weave the remaining swag sections through the knots, extending all the ends evenly. Adjust the swags as desired; tighten knots.

8 Tack all the knots in place.
Knot the end of each swag, leaving 2" (5cm) of the cord to unravel, creating tassels.

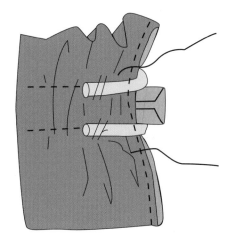

9 Tack the ends of the cord behind each side of the valance, as shown.
Install the valance rod brackets, following manufacturer's instructions. Hang your valance.

Softly Pleated Valance

his valance's gentle cascades frame your window in soft folds of fabric, highlighted by glimpses of the lining underneath. With drapes or on its own, this valance is a graceful addition to any window. The pleats and binding on the upper and lower edges are especially eye-catching. The contrast lining presents an opportunity to use another color or pattern from your decorating scheme.

materials list

◆ 1½ yds. (1.37 m) contrast lining, 54" (137 cm) to 60" (152 cm) wide

◆ 1 yd (91.5 cm) contrast fabric (for binding), 45" (115 cm) to 60" (152 cm) wide

◆ Decorative rod, the length of window width

◆ Six drapery rings, to fit the rod

◆ Six drapery pins

Fabric Suggestions: Medium weight fabrics such as home decorating fabrics, cotton chintz, cotton broadcloth and damask are good choices.

◆ 1½ yds. (1.37 m) fabric, 54" (137 cm) to 60" (152 cm) wide

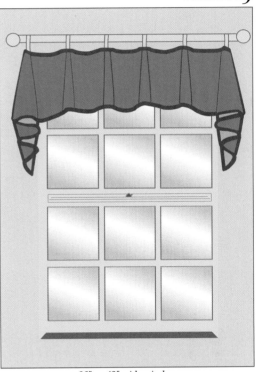

36" or 42" wide window

cutting instructions

1 36" (91.5 cm) Window:
For center, cut one section 45" (115 cm) wide and 16" (40.5 cm) long.
For the sides, cut two sections, each 42" (107 cm) wide and 17" (43 cm) long.

2 42" (107 cm) Window:
For center, cut one section 54" (137 cm) wide and 16" (40.5 cm) long.
For the sides, cut two sections, each 42"(107 cm) wide and 17" (43 cm) long.

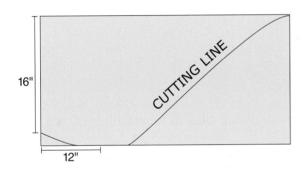

3 Shape side sections, as shown at bottom left.
Starting at the side, make a mark 16" (40.5 cm) from top.
Draw a curve down to the hem approximately 12" (30.5 cm) in from the side; continue, drawing a curve upwards, tapering to a point at the top, as shown.

4 To check the shape you have drawn, trace it onto muslin or tracing paper and pin it in position at the window. A drape or shower curtain may come in handy to pin it to. Mark any adjustments necessary. Use corrected shape to cut side pieces from fabric and lining.

Following instructions on page 95, prepare bias strips.

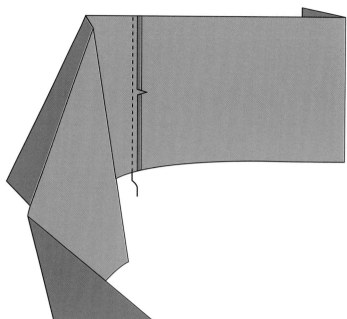

1 With right sides together, stitch one side section to each side of the center section. For the lining, stitch the contrast sections together in the same manner.

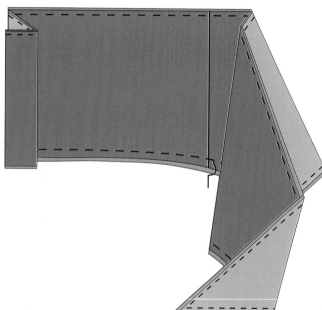

2 With wrong sides together, pin the valance and the lining together, having all edges even. Baste ¼" (6 mm) in from all the outer edges, as shown.

3 Pin the open bias binding to the lining side of the valance, along the upper edge, having raw edges even. Stitch along the upper edge. Press the bias binding toward the seam.

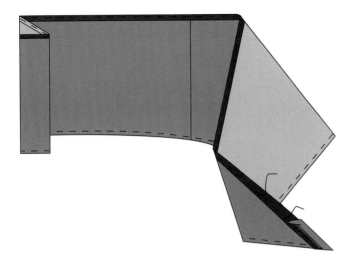

4 Turn the binding to the right side over the seam. Baste the pressed edge over the seam. Edgestitch the pressed edge of the bias binding in place.

5 Complete the binding of the lower curved edge in the same manner as the upper edge, turning in ½" (13 mm) on the raw ends, as shown.

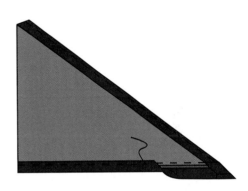

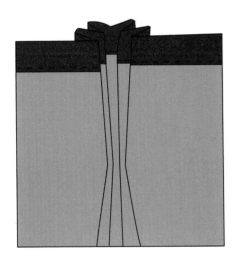

6 Determine pleat locations as follows. For a 36" (91.5 cm) Window: From center of valance, measure 6½" (16.5 cm) in both directions and pin mark. Continue marking 13" (33 cm) from pins to determine location of six pleats. For a 42" (107 cm) Window: Measuring from the center of upper edge measure seven 7" (18 cm) in both directions and pin mark. Continue marking 14" (35.5 cm) from p[ins to determine location of six pleats.
Each pin marks the center of each pleat cluster. Pinch ⅝" (15 mm) on either side. Next, pinch pleats of the same size on either side of the middle pleat. Tack the pleats securely on the lining side of the valance, as shown. Repeat at remaining five pleat markings.

7 Insert a drapery pin into the back of each middle pleat, 1½" (3.8 cm) from upper edge. Insert each drapery pin into a drapery ring.

Install the decorative rod above window, following manufacturer's instructions.

Insert the rod through the rings and hang valance.

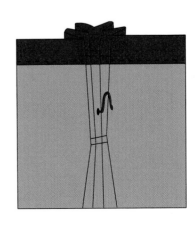

Scalloped Hem Valance

This valance's gentle curves present a subdued silhouette, that is delicate yet confident. Shown in the photo with drapes, this valance also makes a lovely window dressing on its own. It sets a mood that is more relaxed and comfortable than the more dramatic Pointed or Spearpoint designs.

materials list

- ½ yd. (46 cm) fabric, 60" (152 cm) wide

- ½ yd. (46 cm) fabric for lining, 60" (152 cm) wide

- ½ yd. (46 cm) contrast fabric, 45" (115 cm) to 60" (152 cm) wide (for bias trim)

- 1¾ yds. (1.6 m) fusible interfacing, 16" (40.5 cm) wide

- One 1" x 6" (2.5 cm x 15 cm) board the length of window width

- Two angle irons

- Staple gun

Fabric Suggestions: Medium and medium to heavy weight fabrics such as home decorating fabrics, cotton duck, cotton ticking, toile de jouy, damask, linen or even a lightweight tapestry fabric work nicely.

36" or 42" wide window

cutting instructions

1 36" (91.5 cm) Window:
For the valance, cut one section of fabric, 46" (117 cm) wide and 16" (40.5 cm) long.
For valance top, cut one section of fabric, 41" (104 cm) wide and 6½" (16.5 cm) long.
Cut one section of lining, 46" (117 cm) wide and 16" (40.5 cm) long.
Cut one section of fusible interfacing 46" (117 cm) wide and 16" (40.5 cm) long. This is cut on the cross grain.

2 42" (107 cm) Window:
For the valance, cut one section of fabric, 55" (140 cm) wide and 16" (40.5 cm) long.
For the valance top, cut one section of fabric, 47" (120 cm) wide and 6½" (16.5 cm) long.
Cut one section of lining, 55" (140 cm) wide and 16" (40.5 cm) long.
Cut one section of fusible interfacing 55" (140 cm) wide and 16" (40.5 cm) long. This is cut on the cross grain.

3 Using the instructions and template on page 94, shape the lower edge of the valance, the lining and the fusible interfacing.
To cut the contrast bias trim, follow the instructions on page 95.
To shape the ends of the valance top and the mounting board, trace the templates on page 94. Note: The smaller template is for the mounting board.

tips

If you like the coordinated look in your decorating, try using the scallop template to shape the edges of pillows, shams and the comforter in your bedroom or the bottom and sides of your shower curtain.

1 Place the appropriate template on each end of the valance top and mounting board; trace off the curves and cut. (If you do not have access to a saw, most lumberyards and hardware stores will cut wood for a small fee.)

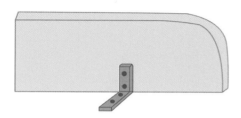

2 Position the board above the upper edge of the window; mark the position of the angle irons on the wall and mounting board. Install the angle irons on the board, following manufacturer's instructions.

3 Fuse the interfacing to the wrong side of the valance.

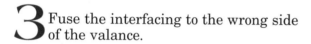

4 With wrong sides together, fold the bias strip in half lengthwise. Press lightly; you do not want to make a crisp crease on the folded edge. Baste the raw edges together.

5 Pin the bias trim to the right side of the lower edge of the valance, having the raw edges of the trim even with the lower edges of the scallops and tapering into inner corners, as shown. Baste the trim in place, approximately ⅜" (10 mm) from the lower edge.

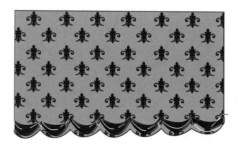

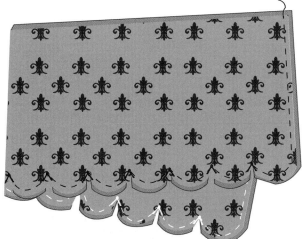

6 With right sides together, pin the lining and the valance together. Stitch the side and lower edges together, pivoting at the inner corners. Clip to the inner corners.

7 Turn the valance right side out. Press the valance, being careful to fully extend the scalloped edges. Baste the upper raw edges together, ½" (13 mm) from the upper edge. Stitch the upper edge 9½" (23.8 cm) in from each side.

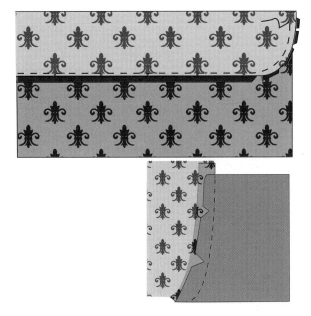

8 With right sides together, pin the upper edge of the valance to the curved edge of the valance top, clipping the upper edge of the valance at the stitching as necessary, ending ½" (13 mm) from the corner of the valance top, as shown. Stitch. Press the seam toward the valance top, turning in the remaining ½" (13 mm) seam allowance.

9 Place the valance on the valance mounting board, lapping the raw edge of the valance top over the back of the board. Staple the valance to the board, as shown. Install the valance over the window at the markings.

Chapter 3

Drapes are so versatile that they are suitable in almost any situation. For the formal dining room, you can make thick, rich drapes of velvet. For a sunroom, breezy, billowing drapes in a pastel print can finish the room with a soft touch. With so many styles to choose from, and fabrics to use, drapes are the perfect palette for your creative impulses.

Tabbed Bordered Drapes are a simple, attractive way to incorporate two different fabrics into your decorating scheme. You might want to choose a print for the border that is highlighted elsewhere in the room. This will not overwhelm the room, but rather tie the drapes to the rest of the room.

materials list

- ◆ 5⅛ yds. (4.7 m) fabric, 45" (115 cm) to 60" (152 cm) wide

- ◆ 2 yds. (1.9 m) contrast fabric, 45" (115 cm) to 60" (152 cm) wide

- ◆ Ten to twelve ⅞" (22 cm) buttons to cover

- ◆ Decorative rod up to 2" (5 cm) diameter and the length of window width or longer if desired.

Fabric Suggestions: Medium weight fabrics, such as home decorating fabrics, denim, silk dupioni, linen and damask, are all great for this style.

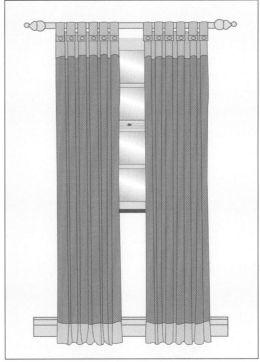

36" or a 42" wide window
Drapes are 90" (229 cm) long.

cutting instructions

1 For the drape panels, cut two sections, each the width of the fabric and 91" (231 cm) long.

2 For the upper and lower bands, cut four sections of the contrast fabric, each the width of the contrast fabric minus 2" (5 cm) and 5" (12.5 cm) long.

3 For the tabs, cut 10 or 12 sections of contrast fabric, each 5" (12.5 cm) wide and 9½" (24 cm) long. The number of tabs you cut depends on your fabric width. For 45" (115 cm) wide fabric, cut ten sections. For 54"/60" (137 cm/152 cm) wide fabric, cut twelve sections.

Save the remaining contrast fabric to cover the buttons.

tips

Layer two sets of drapes, one sheer layer provides privacy, while another more substantial pair blocks out light on those lazy weekend mornings.

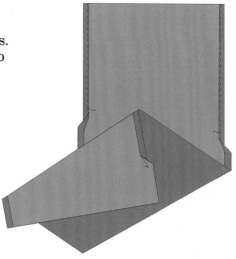

1 Turn in ¾" (20 mm) on the side edges of each panel; press. Turn in side edges ¾"(20 mm) again; press. Stitch close to the inner pressed edges.

2 For the lower bands, turn in ½" (13 mm) on the side edges and one long edge of two band sections; press.

3 Pin the right side of each band section to the wrong side of the lower edge of each panel, having the raw edges even. Stitch the lower edges together.

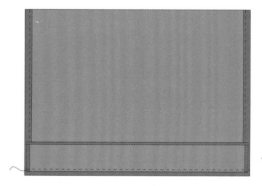

4 Turn the band to the outside along the seam; press. Edgestitch the band in place along the inner pressed edge.

5 With right sides together, fold each tab in half lengthwise. Stitch the side and one end, as shown. Trim.

6 Turn the tabs right side out and press, being careful to get crisp straight edges. Baste the raw edges together.

7 For the upper bands, turn in ½" (13 mm) on the side edges and one long edge of the remaining two band sections; press.

8 Pin the tabs to the right side of the upper band sections, having the raw edges even. Space the tabs evenly along the edge, 7-8" (18-20.5 cm) apart, having the outermost tabs even with the side edges of the band. Baste a scant ½" (13 mm) from the raw edge.

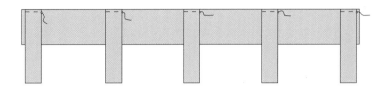

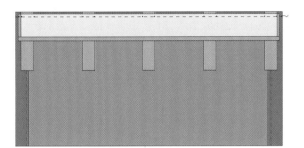

9 Pin the right side of one band to the wrong side of each panel, along the upper edge, having the raw edges even. Stitch the upper edges together.

10 Turn the bands to the outside along the seam; press. Edgestitch the pressed edges in place. On the outside, fold the tabs down, lapping over the upper edge 1½" (3.8 cm). Stitch the tabs close to the upper edge of the panel, as shown.

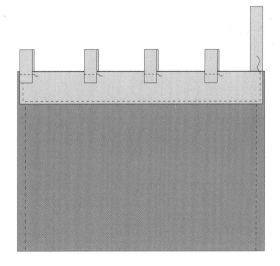

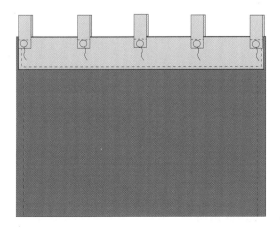

11 Cover the buttons with contrast fabric, following manufacturer's instructions. Sew one button to each tab, making sure to catch the panel with your stitches, to secure the tabs in place.

Install the brackets for your rod at the desired height above the window. Thread the rod through the panel tabs and place the rod on the brackets.

materials list

Fabric Suggestions: Any fabric weight can be used with this style, denim, damask, linen, silk dupioni or upholstery fabrics.

◆ 6⅛ yds. (5.59 m) fabric

◆ One decorative rod, up to 2" (5 cm) diameter and the length of the window width or as desired

36" or a 42" wide window
Drapes are 90" (229 cm) long.

*S*IMPLE TABBED DRAPES are a snap to make! And the simple design means that you are free to experiment with other design elements in creating this window treatment. Choose a dramatic print, a unique fabric or a rod with eye-catching finials.

cutting instructions

1 For the panels, cut two sections of fabric, each the width of the fabric and 99 ½" (253 cm) long.

2 For tabs, cut ten or twelve sections of fabric, each 4½" (11.5 cm) wide and 9" (23 cm) long. The number of tabs you cut depends on your fabric width. For 45" (115 cm) wide fabric, cut ten sections. For 54/60" (137/152 cm) wide fabric, cut twelve sections.

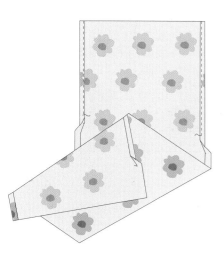

1 Turn in ¾" (20 mm) on the side edges of each panel; press. Turn side edges ¾" (20 mm) again; press. Stitch close to the inner pressed edges.

2 To hem each panel, turn in 2 ½" (6.5 cm) on the lower edge of each panel; press. Turn in 2 ½" (6.5 cm) again; press. Stitch close to the inner pressed edge.

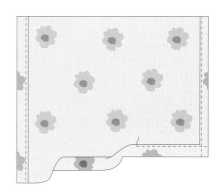

3 With right sides together, fold each tab section in half lengthwise. Stitch the long edges together and leave the ends open.

4 Turn the tabs right side out and press with seam in center back. Baste the raw edges together at each end.

5 Fold each tab in half, as shown, having all the raw edges even. Baste the ends together.

6 To make a facing, turn 4" (10 cm) on the upper edge of each panel to the outside; press. Open out the facing. Pin the tabs to the right side of each panel, placing the raw edges along the pressed crease. Place outermost tabs first, even with side edges. The remaining tabs should be spaced evenly, about 5" - 6" (12.5 - 15 cm) apart. Baste each tab in place, a scant ½" (13 mm) from the raw edge.

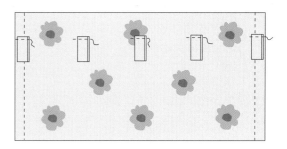

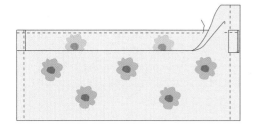

7 With right sides together, fold the facing down along the pressed crease. Stitch ½" (13 mm) from the upper edge, encasing the raw ends of the tabs.

8 Turn the facing to the inside along the seam, turning in ½" (13 mm) on the raw edge; press. Edgestitch the inner pressed edge in place.

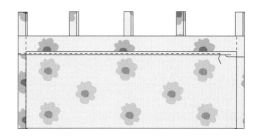

materials list

**Fabric Suggestions:
Light to medium
weight fabrics work
best with this design
because of the bows
such as silk broad-
cloth, chambray or
sheer fabrics, like
organza or voile.**

◆ **7 yds. (6.4 m)
fabric**

◆ **One decorative rod up to 2" (5
cm) diameter and the length
of window width or longer, if
desired**

*36" or 42" wide window
Drapes are 90" (229 cm) long.*

*B*OW TIED DRAPES have a whimsical, light-hearted look. Although made entirely in
pink here, you can also make the bows of a contrast fabric for a different look. You can
also tie the bows differently, or attach decorations to the ends, to create drapes that
are uniquely your own.

cutting instructions

1 For the panels, cut two sections, each
the width of the fabric and 97½" (248
cm) long.

2 For the ties, cut fourteen or sixteen sections of fabric, each 3" (7.5 cm) wide
and 44" (112 cm) long. These should be
cut on the cross grain to save fabric. The number of ties you cut depends on your fabric
width. For 45" (115 cm) wide fabric, cut fourteen sections. For 54"/60" (137/152 cm) wide
fabric, cut sixteen sections.

1 For panel preparation, please refer to the Simple Tabbed Drapes on page 31, steps 1 and 2. Turn in ½" (13 mm) on one end of each tie; press. With right sides together, fold each tie in half lengthwise. Stitch the raw edges together, leaving the pressed edge open. Trim.

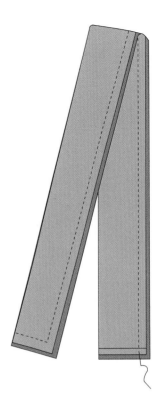

2 Turn the ties right side out and press, producing crisp straight edges. Slipstitch the open ends of each tie together.

3 For the facing, turn down 4" (10 cm) on the upper edge of each panel to the outside; press. Open out the facing.

Fold each tie in half. Pin the ties to the right side of each panel, placing the folded edge of each tie along the crease. Baste each tab in place, a scant ½" (13 mm) from the folded edge.

To complete the panels, please refer to Simple Tabbed Drapes, page 31, steps 7 and 8.

Install the brackets for your rod at the desired height above the window. Tie the ties around the rod and place the rod on the brackets.

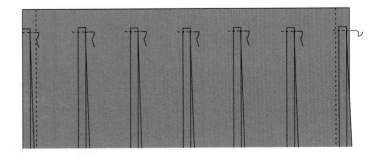

36" or a 42" wide window
Drapes are 90" long.

materials list

Fabric Suggestions: Medium weight fabrics, such as home decorating fabrics, linen, denim, ticking and toile de joie.

◆ **6 ½ yds. (5.49 m) fabric**

◆ **9 yds. (8.49 m) cord (for piping)**

◆ **1 ⅜ yds. (1.26 m) contrast fabric (for piping)**

◆ **Ten to twelve ⅞" (22 cm) buttons to cover**

BUTTON TABBED DRAPES have a tailored look that is still casual and relaxed. The piping around the edges picks up just a hint of contrast color, and the buttons are an eye-catching addition. The drapes pictured here are more subtle — perfect for a busy family room. But made of denim, they are a fun and unique treatment for a child's bedroom.

cutting instructions

1 For the drape panels, cut two sections, each the width of the fabric and 99½" (253 cm) long.

2 For the tabs, cut twenty or twenty-four sections of fabric, each 3½" (9 cm) wide and 11½" (29.2 cm) long. The number of tabs you cut depends on the width of your fabric. For 45" (115 cm) wide fabric, cut twenty sections. For 54" /60" (137/152 cm) wide fabric, cut twenty-four sections.

3 One end of each tab needs to be shaped. Please refer to page 94 for the template and instructions.

For bias preparation for the piping, please refer to page 95.

Save the remaining contrast fabric to cover the buttons.

1 For panel preparation, please refer to the Simple Tabbed Drapes on page 31, steps 1 and 2. Prepare bias strips.

To make the piping, center the cord over the wrong side of the bias strip, having the ends even, as shown. Then, fold the bias strip over the cord, keeping long raw edges even. Stitch close to the cord, using a zipper foot. Trim excess fabric along the raw edge to a scant ½" (13 mm) between the stitching and the raw edge.

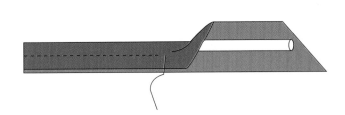

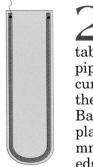 

2 On the right side of half the tab sections, pin piping to sides and curved end, having the raw edges even. Baste the piping in place, a scant ½" (13 mm) from the raw edges.

3 With right sides together, pin one remaining tab section to each tab with piping, having all the edges even. Using a zipper foot, stitch a generous ½" (13 mm) from raw edge, leaving the upper edge open. Clip the seam allowances.

4 Turn each tab right side out. Press the tabs, being careful to extend the piping. Baste the raw edges together.

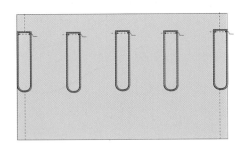

5 For the facing, turn down 4" (10 cm) on the upper edge of each panel to the outside; press. Open out the facing. Pin the tabs to the right side of the panel, placing the raw edges along the crease. The outermost tabs should be even with the side edges of the panel. Space the remaining tabs evenly, approximately 5-6" (12.5-15 cm) apart. Baste each tab a scant ½" from the raw edge.

6 To complete the panels, please refer to Simple Tabbed Drapes page 31, Steps 7 and 8.

7 Fold the tabs to the right side of the panel, having the curved ends extending 3" (7.5 cm) over upper edge. Pin them in place. Cover the buttons with the remaining contrast fabric. Sew one button to each tab, making sure to catch the panel, to secure the tabs in place.

Install the brackets for your rod at the desired height above the window. Thread the rod through the tabs and place the rod on the brackets.

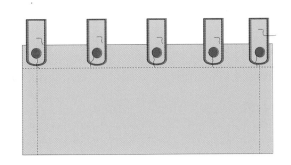

Reversibles

These completely reversible window dressings offer twice as many decorating choices! It's just a matter of one quick flip to change the color, texture or attitude of your windows in minutes. A limitless number of combinations can be had with all the different choices of fabrics; a contrast of light and dark, subtle and bold, plain and patterned or textured and smooth to name just a few.

Double Scalloped Valance works equally well with large and small prints. The bold shape of the scallops carries off a variety of looks, from country kitchen to modern living room. This photo shows a decidedly country look, but if you made this window dressing out of silk damask and silk broadcloth, and tied it with velvet or organza ribbons, it would do very well in a home with contemporary decor.

materials list

◆ 1 yd. (91.5 cm) fabric, 54" (137 cm) to 60" (152 cm) wide

◆ 1 yd. (91.5 cm) contrast fabric (for reverse side), 54" (137 cm) to 60" (152 cm) wide

◆ 5 yds. (4.6 m) of 1½" (3.8 cm) grosgrain ribbon

◆ One 1½" (3.8 cm) diameter decorative rod

Fabric suggestions: Any weight of fabric except very light works well. Try cotton chintz, home decorating fabrics, cotton homespun, damask, linen, denim, silk dupioni or cotton toile.

36"(91.5 cm) and 48"(122 cm) wide windows.

cutting instructions

1 For the valance, cut one section of fabric the width of the window plus 1" (25 mm) and 32" (81 cm) long.

2 For the contrast lining, cut one section of contrast fabric, in the same manner as the fabric.

Please refer to the template and instructions on page 94 to shape the top and lower edges of the valance and the valance contrast lining.

tips

The clear lines of the double scalloped valance are like a blank canvas. Try perhaps a painted scene on cotton duck or a pieced crazy quilt as one of the fabrics?

Also, in both these photographs, the contrast is invisible, so you could hang this window dressing back to front ~ without any contrast showing at the lower edge.

1 With right sides together, stitch the outer edges of the valance and the contrast lining together, pivoting at the inner corners and leaving a 6" (15 cm) opening on one side for turning. Trim and clip.

2 Turn the valance right side out. Press the valance, being careful to fully extend seams so scallops are rounded smoothly. Slipstitch the opening closed. (*)

To form casings, first fold the valance, having the sides even and scallops 3½" (9 cm) apart; press lightly to make a soft crease. Open out the valance and stitch 3" (7.5 cm) and 4½" (11.5 cm) from either side of the crease. Press out the crease. Open the side seams between the stitching, as shown.

3 Cut two pieces of ribbon, each 72" (185 cm) for a 36" (91.5 cm) window or 90" (229 cm) for a 48" (122 cm) window. Insert the ribbons through the casings.

Install the brackets for your rod at the desired height above the window, following manufacturer's instructions.

To hang the valance, lay the valance over the rod, having the casing spaced evenly on each side of the rod. Tie the ribbons at each end into bows.

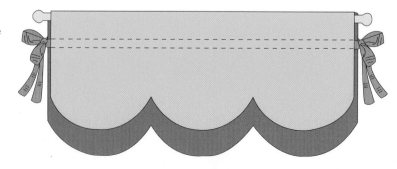

Variation

The Double Scalloped Valance's second fabric acts more as a high-light, and the bows along the rod are a fun touch.

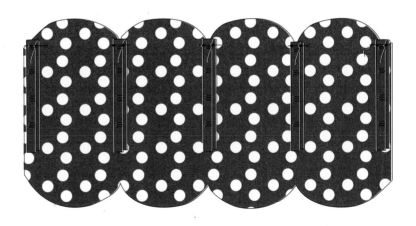

1 For the construction of this valance variation, please refer to page 38, step 1 up to (*) in step 2.

Cut five pieces of ribbon, each 32" (81 cm) long. Fold each piece of ribbon in half and pin to valance, centering at inner corners and extending folded edge ½" (13 mm) past valance edge, as shown. Stitch securely ⅝" (15 mm) from the folded edge. Press the ribbons upward.

2 To hang the valance, tie the ribbons to the rod and place the rod on the brackets.

Double Pointed Valance

Although similiar to the Double Scalloped Valance, this design presents a bolder appearance. Shown here, the pairing of these two fabrics lets us play stripe against print to create this crisp cheerful look. But you can also consider making them of a tapestry fabric, or heraldic print, for a grander impression.

materials list

- 1⅛ yds. (103 cm) fabric, 54" (137 cm) to 60" (152 cm) wide

- 1⅛ yds. (103 cm) contrast fabric (for the reverse side), 54" (137 cm) to 60" (152 cm) wide

- 5 yds. (4.6 m) 1½" (3.8 cm) grosgrain ribbon

- One 1½" (3.8 cm) diameter decorative rod the length of the window width or as desired.

Fabric Suggestions: Any weight except very light fabric suits this bold style. Home decorating fabrics, cotton duck, denim, polished cotton, cotton pique and chintz are all good choices.

36" (91.5 cm) and 48" (122 cm) wide window

cutting instructions

1 For the valance, cut one section of fabric the width of your window plus 1" (25 mm) and 36" (91.5 cm) long.

2 For contrast lining, cut one section of contrast fabric, in the same manner as the fabric.

Please refer to the template and instructions on page 94 to shape the edges of the valance and the valance contrast lining.

Note: Be sure to trace the template on opposite ends of the valance so that points alternate.

tips

Though we show the large points of this valance without any trim, it is easy to add trim. Just remember, as this valance is reversible, you will hand sew the trim on both sides. It is possible to use fringe or any trim that hangs below the lower edge, just make sure that you like it with both fabrics as it shows when the valance is reversed.

1 With right sides together, stitch the outer edges of the valance and the valance contrast lining together, pivoting at the inner corners and leaving a 6" (15 cm) opening for turning. Trim and clip.

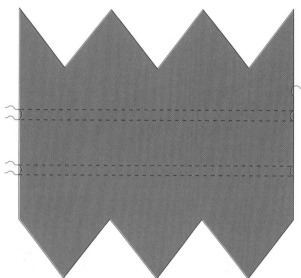

2 Turn the valance right side out. Press the valance, being careful to fully extend the seams so that the sides are straight and points are nicely formed. Slipstitch the opening closed. (*)

To form casings, first fold the valance in half, having the sides even; press lightly to make a soft crease. Open out the valance and stitch 3" (7.5 cm) and 4½" (11.5 cm) from either side of the crease. Press out the crease. Open the side seams between the rows of stitching, as shown.

3 Cut two pieces of ribbon, each 72" (185 cm) for a 36" (91.5 cm) window or 90" (229 cm) for a 48" (122 cm) window. Insert the ribbons through the casings.

Install the brackets for your rod at the desired height above the window, following manufacturer's instructions.

To hang the valance, lay the valance over the rod, having the casings spaced evenly on each side of the rod. Tie the ribbons at each end into bows.

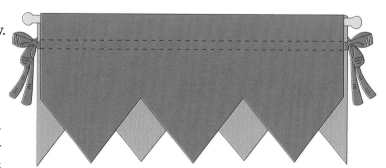

Variation

The Double Pointed Valance is quite cheerful. The tiny triangles are reminiscent of folded handkerchiefs, and the soft bows are a nice complement to the pointed edges.

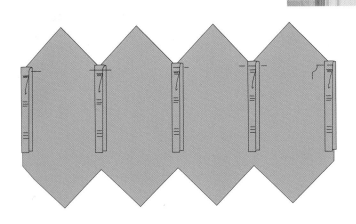

1 For the construction of this valance variation, please refer to Double Pointed Valance, page 42, steps 1 and step 2 up to (*).

Cut five pieces of ribbon, each 32" (81 cm) long. Fold each piece of ribbon in half and pin to the valance, centering at the inner corners and extending folded edge ½" (13 mm) past valance edge, as shown. Stitch the ribbon to the valance securely ⅝" (15 mm) from the folded edge. Press the ribbons upward.

2 To hang the valance, tie the ribbons to the rod.

Turnback Drapes

These drapes, though simple to make, give easy grace and charm to any room. Designed to remain stationery, the sides are held back by covered buttons which can be quickly released for privacy. And, as there are two buttons on each side, two different looks can be achieved. As pictured here, the drapes are lively and bright, made of contrasting prints in the same color palette, but other combinations work equally as well.

*I*n the reverse picture here we see how easily the drapes can be reversed to give this decorating scheme a different feel. Even more versatility can be achieved if we combine two
fabrics with a greater degree of contrast of design — or perhaps keep one fabric plain?

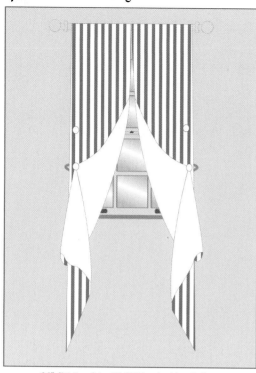

*36" (91.5 cm) to 42" (107 cm) wide window.
Drapes are 90" (229 cm) long.*

materials list

Fabric Suggestions:
Medium weight fabrics,
such as cotton duck,
denim, light weight can-
vas, velvet, satin, cor-
duroy, damask, linen and
silk do well here.

◆ 5½ yds. (4.57 m) fabric,
45" (115 cm) to 60" (152
cm) wide

◆ 5½ yds. (4.57 m) contrast
fabric, 45" (115 cm) to
60" (152 cm) wide

◆ Eight 1⅛" (2.8 cm) but-
tons to cover

◆ Four ½" (13 mm) plastic
rings

◆ **Two cup hooks**

◆ 1" (25 mm) decorative
rod the length of win-
dow width or as
desired.

cutting instructions

1 For the drape panels, cut two sections
of fabric, each half the width of your
window, plus 1" (25 mm) and 91" (231
cm) long.

2 Save the remaining fabric to cover the
buttons.

Prepare the contrast lining in the same manner.

tips

Though we show this window dressing with
plain edges here, create another great look by
trimming the edges with ball fringe or decorative braid and substituting decorative buttons
for the covered buttons.

As this is a stationary window treatment, you
might want to pair these drapes with a shade
for light and privacy. A coordinated shade,
using your drape fabric and a shade kit pro-
duces either a very cozy or opulent look,
depending on the fabrics you choose.

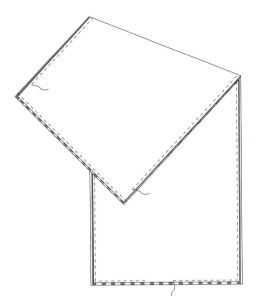

1 With right sides together, pin one fabric panel to each contrast fabric panel, having all the edges even. Stitch all around the edges, leaving the sides open between ½" (13 mm) and 2½" (6.5 cm) from the upper edge and leaving an opening for turning at the lower edge. Trim corners.

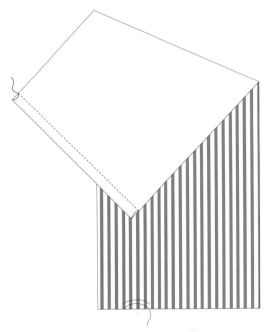

2 Turn each panel right side out. Press the panel, making crisp corners and straight edges. Slipstitch the opening at the lower edge closed. To form a casing in each panel, stitch across the panel, 2" (5 cm) from the upper edge (at break in previous stitching), as shown.

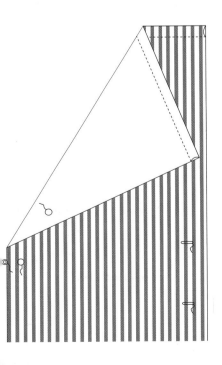

3 On each panel, make buttonholes in 1" (25 mm) from the inner side edges and 37½" (95 cm) and 48" (122 cm) below the upper edge.

For the button placement, mark the panel along the outer edge, 29" (74 cm) and 41" (104 cm) below the upper edge.
Cover eight buttons, four of fabric and four of contrast fabric, following manufacturer's instructions.
Sew contrasting buttons to both sides of the panels at the markings.
Sew a plastic ring to the outer edge of each panel, opposite the lower button on each side.

Install the brackets for your rod at the desired height above the window, following manufacturer's instructions.
Thread the rod through the panels and place on the bracket.
Insert the cup hooks into the window frame opposite the plastic rings. Hook the rings onto the cup hooks.
Create turnbacks by buttoning inside edge to outside button.

Curved Valance Café Curtains

Curved Valance Café Curtains are very easy to make yet they accent a window perfectly. The valance accents the frame and the curtains provide privacy while letting in plenty of sunlight. Constructed of cheerful coordinating cottons, these playful, sunny curtains brighten up the baby's room. Depending upon your choice of fabric, these versatile curtains suit any room.

Switch sides and you can change the tone of the room to a slightly more sophisticated look. This works very well for a child's bedroom — a print suitable for an infant on one side and then a more mature look for the reverse.

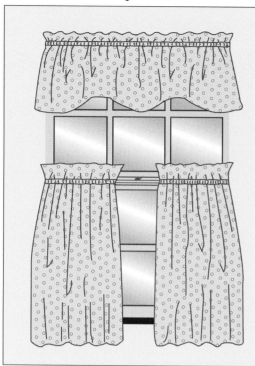

Up to 60" (152 cm) wide window, 60" long

materials list

Fabric Suggestions: Any light or medium weight fabric. Try contrasting or coordinating fabrics, such as cotton chintz, polished cotton, light weight denim or chambray, seersucker, gingham or linen.

◆ **3⅜ yds. (3.1 m) fabric, 45" (115 cm) to 60" (152 cm) wide**

◆ **3⅜ yds. (3.1 m) contrast fabric, 45" (115 cm) to 60" (152 cm) wide**

◆ **Two 1" (25 mm) extension rods with a 1" (25 mm) return**

cutting instructions

1 Valance:

For the center of the valance, cut one piece of fabric 44" (112 cm) wide and 18" (46 cm) long.

For the sides of the valance, cut two pieces of fabric, each 30" (76 cm) wide and 18" (46 cm) long.

Stitch one side section to each side of the center section.

With right sides together, fold the valance in half lengthwise.

To shape the lower edge, it is possible to draw upon the fabric directly or make a template of paper. If you elect to draw upon the fabric directly, use chalk or a disappearing pen, to avoid any drawing showing through to the right side.

The distance from the highest point of the curve to the fold is 24" (61 cm).

The height of the curve is 5" (12.5 cm).

Once you have drawn the lines following the measurements above, draw a gentle curve, as

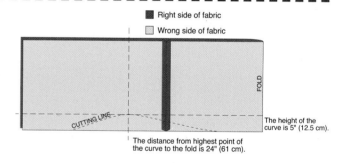

Right side of fabric

Wrong side of fabric

FOLD

CUTTING LINE

The height of the curve is 5" (12.5 cm).

The distance from highest point of the curve to the fold is 24" (61 cm).

shown. Cut the curve.

For the contrast valance, prepare the contrast fabric in the same manner.

2 Curtains:

For the curtain panels, cut two sections of fabric, each the width of the fabric and 31" (78.5 cm) long.

For the contrast curtain panels, cut two sections of contrast fabric, each the width of the fabric above and 31" (78.5 cm) long.

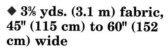

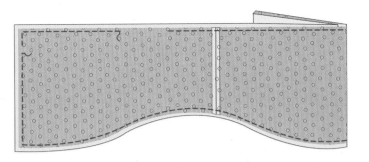

1 With right sides together, pin the valance and the contrast valance together, having all the edges even. Stitch, leaving the sides open between 2" (5 cm) and 3½" (9 cm) from the upper edge and an opening along the upper edge for turning. Trim corners and clip curves.

2 Turn the valance right side out and press, creating a smooth curve at the lower edge. Slipstitch the opening on the upper edge closed. To form the casing, stitch 1½" (6.5 cm) and 3" (7.5 cm) from the upper edge, as shown.

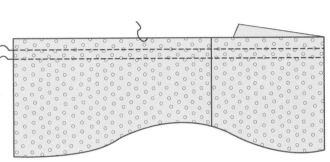

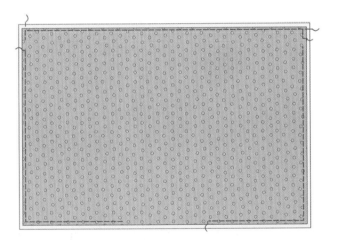

3 With right sides together, pin one curtain panel to each contrast curtain panel. Stitch, leaving the sides open between 2" (5 cm) and 3½" (9 cm) from the upper edge and an opening on the lower edge for turning. Trim corners.

4 Turn the curtain panels right side out. Press the panels, to make crisp edges and corners.
To form the casing, stitch each panel 1½" (3.8 cm) and 3" (7.5 cm) from the upper edge.
Install the brackets for the extension rods at the desired height on the window frame, following the manufacturer's instructions.
Thread the rods through the casings of the valance and curtain panels. Place the rods on the brackets. Arrange the fullness of the valance and curtains as desired.

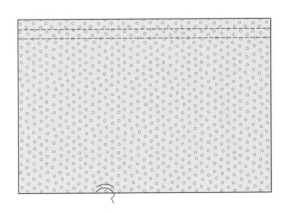

Chevron Valance Café Curtains

This design pairs the strong shape of the chevron with easy-to-make curtains. They cover the window sufficiently for privacy, yet allow a good amount of light in the window. This set of curtains has a very crisp attitude, trimmed in cord. However, the application of fringe or another trim with a softer edge to a less graphic fabric creates an entirely different, softer look.

The reverse of these curtains, is much lighter and brighter in appearance. A way to bring even more light in, is to attach a prism at the center point of the valance – or attach prisms along the lower edge of the valance. Whatever you choose, if you plan to use trim that hangs below the lower edge of a reversible window dressing, make sure that it complements both fabrics.

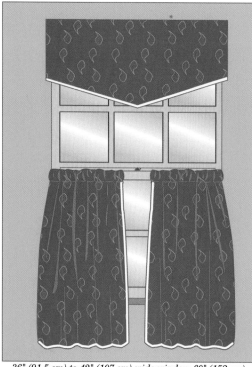

36" (91.5 cm) to 42" (107 cm) wide window, 60" (152 cm)

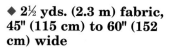

materials list

Fabric Suggestions: A crisp fabric of any weight except very heavy will do. Choose from denim, polished cotton, linen, damask, pique, corduroy or silk dupioni.

◆ 2½ yds. (2.3 m) fabric, 45" (115 cm) to 60" (152 cm) wide

◆ 2½ yds. (2.3 m) contrast fabric, 45" (115 cm) to 60" (152 cm) wide.

◆ 7 yds. (6.4 m) ⅜" (10 mm) decorative cord with lip

◆ Two 1" (25 mm) extension rods with a 1" (25 mm) return

cutting instructions

1 Valance:
Cut one piece of fabric, the width of the window, plus 3" (7.5 cm) and 16" (40.5 cm) long. For instance, for a 36" (91.5 cm) window, cut one piece of fabric 39" (99 cm) wide and 16" (40.5 cm) long.

With right sides together, fold the valance in half with selvages together. At the selvage, mark 10" (25.5 cm) down from the upper edge. Draw a line from that mark to the lower edge at the fold. Cut along the drawn line.

Prepare the contrast valance in the same manner as the fabric valance.

■ Right side of fabric

□ Wrong side of fabric

2 Curtains:
Cut two sections of fabric, each the width of the fabric and 31" (78.5 cm) long.
Cut two sections of contrast fabric, each the width of the fabric above and 31" (78.5 cm) long.

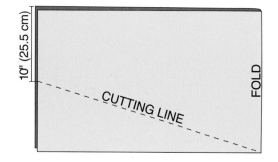

10" (25.5 cm)

CUTTING LINE

FOLD

1 With right sides together, pin the cord with lip to the lower edge of the valance, placing the lip along the raw edges and tapering the ends into the sides, as shown. Baste the cord with lip in place.

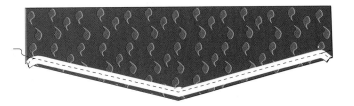

2 With right sides together, pin the contrast valance to the valance, having all the edges even. Stitch, using a zipper foot, leaving the side edges open between ½" (13 mm) and 2" (5 cm) from the upper edge and an opening on the upper edge for turning.

3 Turn the valance right side out. Press the valance, making sure to extend the cord with lip fully from the seam and creating a crisp point at the center. Slipstitch the opening at the upper edge closed.

4 With right sides together, pin the cord with lip to the inner and lower edges of each curtain panel, placing the lip along the raw edge, tapering the end on the inner side of the panel ½" (13 mm) from the upper edge and the remaining end ½" (13 mm) from the side edge. Baste the cord with lip in place. Clip the cord with lip at the corner.

5 With right sides together, pin one contrast curtain panel to each curtain panel. Stitch, using a zipper foot, leaving openings on the side edges between ½" (13 mm) and 2" (5 cm) from the upper edge and an opening at the upper edge for turning.

6 Turn each curtain panel right side out and press, fully extending the cord at the edges and the corner. Slipstitch the opening on the upper edge closed. For the casing, stitch 1½" (3.8 cm) from the upper edge. To form a casing, stitch 1½" (3.8 cm) from the upper edge. Install the brackets for the rods, following manufacturer's instructions. Thread the valance and curtains onto the rods and place them on the brackets.

Chapter 5

Panels are ideal for a room that needs a subtle decorating touch. They are designed to fit within the moldings, and thus accent a window or door simply yet elegantly. This is a perfect way to highlight other aspects of your decor, such as attractive moldings, special wallpapers or paint colors. Made here of textured sheer fabrics, these panels provide just the right combination of privacy and light.

Sheer Overlay Door Panels are a refreshing new way to dress a door panel or any tall narrow window. Though these panels provide complete coverage, they are supported by adjustable crane rods which swing open to instantly reveal the view.

materials list

- ◆ **2 yds. (1.83 m) fabric, 45" (115 cm) to 60" (152 cm)**
- ◆ **2 yds. (1.83 m) contrast fabric, 45" (115 cm) to 60" (152 cm)**
- ◆ **One pair of adjustable crane rods**

Fabric Suggestions: Sheer fabrics, such as batiste, organza, and voile make the best of the double layered design.

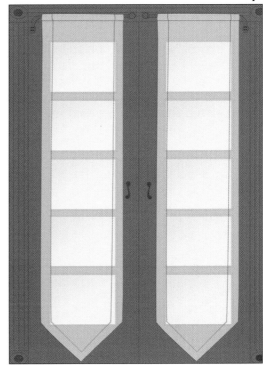

Panels 13" (33 cm) wide and 90" (229 cm) long.

cutting instructions

1 For the panels, cut two pieces of fabric, each 15" (38 cm) wide and 93½" (237 cm) long.

2 To shape the lower edge of the panel, with right sides together, fold the panel in half lengthwise.
Measure 7" (18 cm) up from the lower edge at the side; mark.
Draw a line from the mark to the fold at the lower edge; cut along the line.

3 For the contrast overlay sections, cut two pieces of contrast fabric, each 10" (25.5 cm) wide and 83½" (212 cm) long.
Prepare the overlay sections as in step 2.

■ Right side of fabric
□ Wrong side of fabric

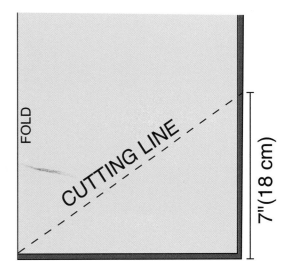

FOLD

CUTTING LINE

7"(18 cm)

1 Turn in ½" (13 mm) on the side and lower
edges of each panel and contrast overlay
section; press the edges. Turn in ½" (13 mm)
again on the side and lower edges; press. Sew or
hand stitch the inner pressed edges in place.

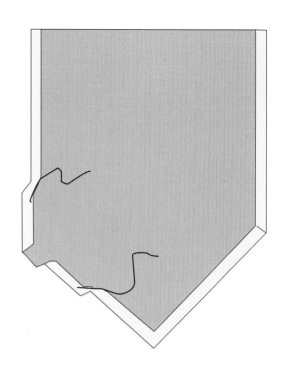

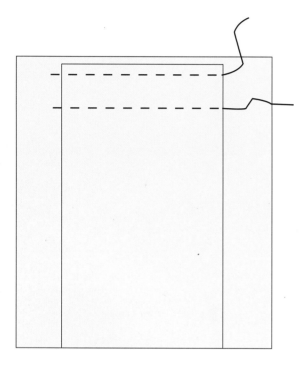

2 Center and pin the wrong side of each overlay to the right side of each panel, having
the upper edges even. Baste the upper raw edges
together and then again 2" (5 cm) below.

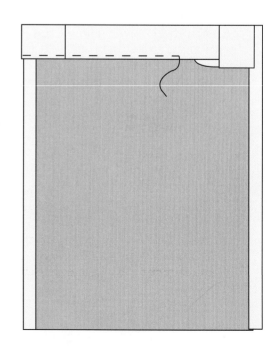

3 To form the casing, turn in the upper edge
2½" (6.5 cm), turning in ½" (13 mm) on the
raw edge; press. Stitch close to the inner pressed
edge.

Install the adjustable crane rods on the door or
window frame, following manufacturer's instructions.

Thread panels onto rods and hang over windows.

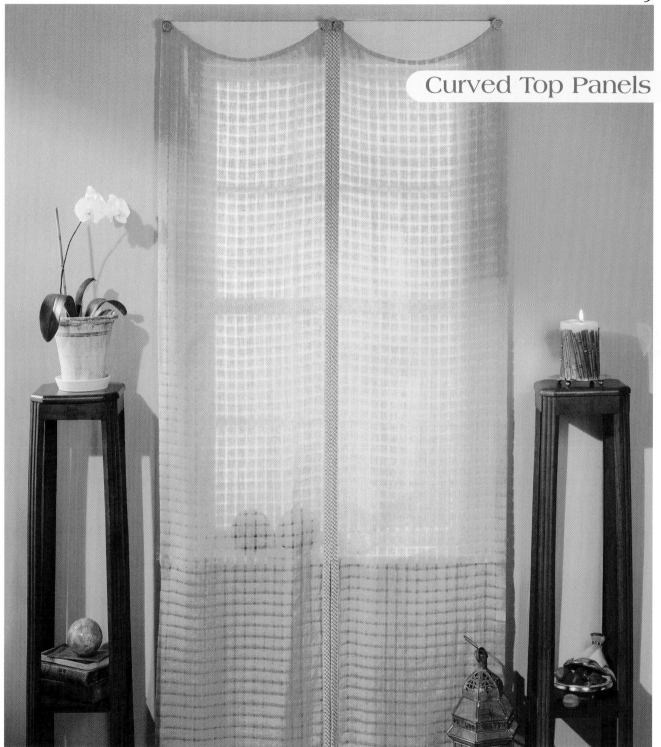

Curved Top Panels

These stationary panels are trimmed with foldover braid, giving them vertical emphasis. The jaunty curve at the top softens the look, and the drapery push pins are an added adornment. All these elements, together with the open weave fabric, make a casual, yet classic, window dressing.

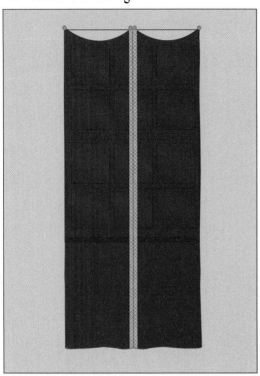

Window up to 42" wide. Panels 90" (229 cm) long.

materials list

Fabric Suggestions: Light weight open weave fabrics, lace or sheer fabrics, such as organza are best.

◆ 2¼ yds. (2.52 m) fabric, 45" (115 cm) to 60" (152 cm) wide

◆ 5¼ yds. (4.98 m) foldover braid

◆ Four drapery push pins

cutting instructions

1 For the panels, cut two sections of fabric, each half the width of the window plus 3" and 97½" (248 cm) long.

2 To shape the upper edge, with right sides together, fold each panel in half lengthwise.

From the upper outside corner, draw a curve down to 3" (7.5 cm) from upper edge at the fold. Cut along that curve.

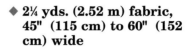

■ Right side of fabric☐

□ Wrong side of fabric

3" (7.5cm)

CUTTING LINE

tips

If you find all available drapery push pins a bore, don't hesitate to enhance them yourself. Glue on your own exciting additions ~ like silk flowers, beads or seashells.

1 Turn in ¾" (20 cm) on the side edges of each
panel; press. Turn in ¾" (20 cm) again; press.
Sew or handstitch the inner pressed edges in place.

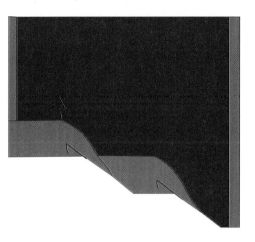

2 Turn in 3¼" (8.2 cm) on the lower edge of
each panel; press. Turn in 3¼" (8.2 cm)
again; press. Sew or handstitch the inner
pressed edge in place.

3 Turn in ½" (13 mm) on the upper edge of each
panel and press. Turn in ½" (13 mm) again; press.
Sew or handstitch the inner pressed edge in place.

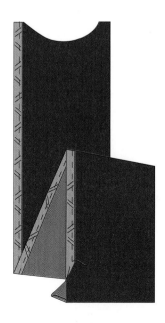

4 Encase the inner side edge of each panel with foldover
braid, placing the narrower edge of the braid on the
right side of the panel and turning in ½" (13 mm) on the
ends. On the right side, stitch close to the inner edge of the
braid

Mount the panels on the window with the drapery push
pins.

Curved Valance Café Panels

These airy café panels provide privacy without depriving you of sunlight. This photo shows a lighthearted approach with open weave fabric and cotton fringe. But imagine this set of panels in a burnout velvet and beaded fringe-- you would find this a delightful addition to a Victorian decorating scheme.

materials list

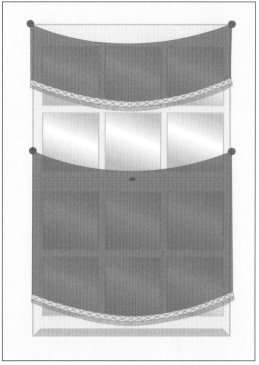

◆ 1½ yds. (1.37 m) fabric, 45" (155 cm) to 60" (152 cm) wide

◆ 2½ yds. (2.29 m) fringe trim

◆ Four drapery push pins

Fabric Suggestions: Sheer and open weave fabrics, such as cotton voile, batiste, silk organza, and gauze are all good choices. Also suitable for heavier fabrics such as burnout velvet.

Window up to 42" (107 cm) wide and 60" (152 cm) long.

cutting instructions

1 For the upper panel, cut one section of fabric the width of the window plus 2" (5 cm) and 16" (40.5 cm) long.
For the lower panel, cut one section of fabric the same width as above and 36" (91.5 cm) long.

■ Right side of fabric

□ Wrong side of fabric

2 To shape the upper and lower edges of the panels, fold each panel, right sides together, in half lengthwise.
For the lower edge, draw a curve from outer edge, 3" (7.5 cm) up from lower edge to the fold at the lower edge; cut along that curve.
For the upper edge of each panel, similarly, draw a curve from upper outside corner to 3" (7.5 cm) down from upper edge at the fold; cut along that curve.

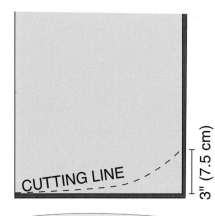

CUTTING LINE

3" (7.5 cm)

tips

Before buying your full yardage of fabric, take home a swatch to check how the color and pattern looks with the rest of your decor ~ in day and evening light.

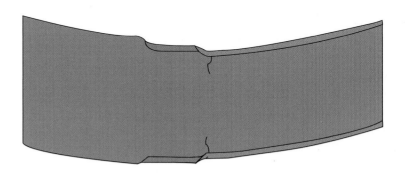

1 Turn in ½" (13 mm) on the upper and lower edges of each panel and press. Turn in ½" (13 mm) again; press. Sew or handstitch inner pressed edge in place.

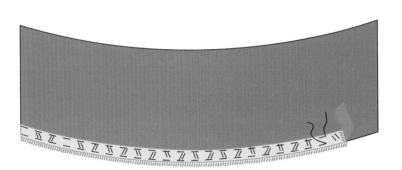

2 On the outside, pin the fringe trim to the lower edge of each panel, having the heading of the trim even with the lower edge of the panel and ends even with the side edges. Stitch the trim to the panel along both long edges of the trim heading.

Turn in ½" (13 mm) on the side edges of each panel and press. Turn in ½" (13 mm) again; press. Sew or handstitch close to the inner pressed edges.

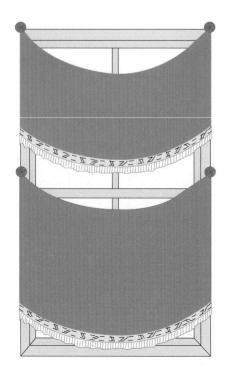

3 Mount the panels on the window frame with the drapery push pins.

Sheer Overlay Café Panels

These stationary panels showcase a deeply textured sheer fabric. For those who are collectors of antique fabrics, this is a perfect way to exhibit your finds. What better way to use a treasured wedding gown or lace tablecloth, than as a layer in this graceful treatment? Also, here we see a play of light against dark. These very easy panels can also be done in tone on tone fabrics for a subtle presentation.

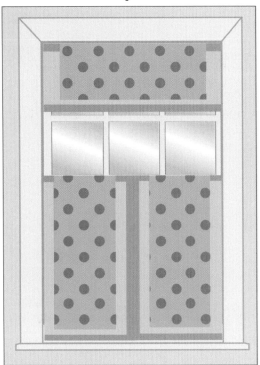

Window 36" (91.5 cm) wide and 60" (152 cm) long.

materials list

Fabric Suggestions: Lace, organza, batiste, organdy, embellished organza or any sheer fabrics are terrific choices for this window dressing.

◆ **1½ yds. (1.38 m) fabric, 45" (115 cm) to 60" (152 cm) wide**

◆ **1⅜ yds. (1.25 m) contrast fabric, 45" (115 cm) to 60" (152 cm) wide**

◆ **Two tension rods, the length of window width inside molding**

cutting instructions

1 For the upper panel, cut one section of fabric 38" (96.5 cm) wide and 14½" (37 cm) long.
For the lower panels, cut two sections of fabric, each 20" (51 cm) wide and 33½" (85 cm) long.

2 For the upper contrast overlay, cut one section of contrast fabric 32" (81 cm) wide and 12" (30.5 cm) long.
For the lower contrast overlays, cut two sections of contrast fabric, each 14" (35.5 cm) wide and 31" (78.5 cm) long.

tips

You may be surprised to hear that a handy tool for your work table is ~ an ashtray! Select a heavy-weight ashtray, and use it to hold your pins and marking pencil, as well as keep your fabric in place. Look for one made of material that is both sturdy and decorative, such as glass, marble or stone.

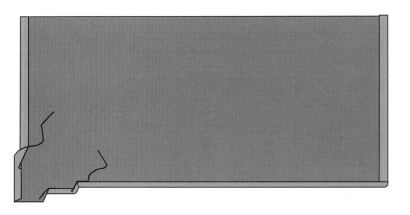

1 Turn in ½" (13 mm) on the side and lower edges of each of the panels and contrast overlay sections; press. Turn in ½" (13 mm) again and press. Sew or handstitch the inner pressed edges in place.

2 Center and pin the wrong side of the upper overlay section to the right side of the upper panel, having the upper edges even. Baste close to the upper raw edges and 2 ¼" (5.7 cm) below.

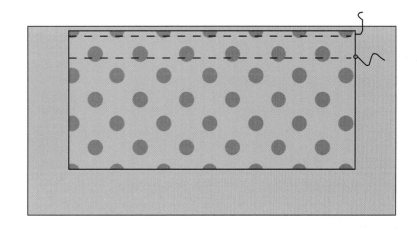

3 To form the casing, turn in the upper edge of the panel along the inner basting, turning in ½" (13 mm) on the raw edge. Stitch close to the inner pressed edge.

Prepare the lower panels and lower contrast overlay sections in the same manner as above.

To hang the panels, thread the panels onto the tension rods and place the rods in the window frame as we show in the photograph on page 65.

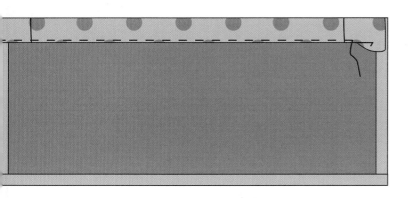

Tucked Sheer Shade

This versatile stationary window dressing suits any room. Here we see this shade in a kitchen, made of a sheer cotton batiste. The horizontal lines of the design are bold, yet the sheer fabric presents an image of delicacy. You might want a stationary treatment such as this for a ground floor window that needs constant coverage, or one that is out of reach, and that you do not often open.

materials list

◆ 3⅛ yds. (2.85 m) fabric, 45" (115 cm) to 60" (152 cm) wide

◆ One tension rod the length of window width inside moldings

Fabric Suggestions: Any light or mid weight sheer fabric, such as cotton batiste, handkerchief linen, embellished silk organza or cotton voile makes a fine shade.

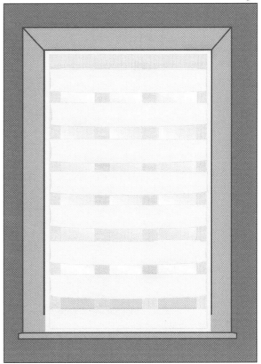

Window up to 42" (107 cm) wide.
Window 60" (152 cm) long.

cutting instructions

1 Cut one section the width of the window inside the moldings plus 2" (5 cm) and 112½" (286.5 cm) long.

2 For a tuck template, rule lines on a series of paper the length of the shade 112½" (286.5 cm) long, starting 16½" (42 cm) from the top, mark six 6½" (16.5 cm) tucks at 8" (20.5 cm) intervals, leaving 14½" (37 cm) unmarked at the bottom.

tips

For added flair, flat items such as silk flowers and leaves can be inserted into the tucks. Or, insert ribbons or trim. If the fabric you chose is very sheer, even photographs can be placed within the tucks.

Use items that do not weigh very much as you do not want to distort the crisp lines of this window dressing design.

To further accentuate the tucks, sew trim at the lower edge of each tuck. A flat braid, ribbon or tape does nicely.

1 Lightly transfer these lines to the wrong side of the shade.

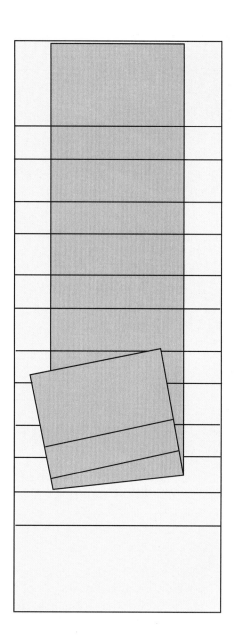

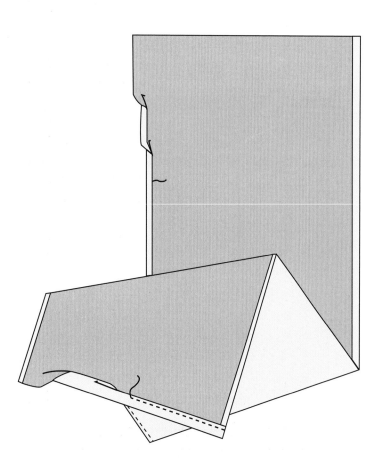

2 Turn in ½" (13 mm) on the side edges of the shade and press. Turn in ½" (13 mm) again; press. Sew or handstitch inner pressed edge in place.
Turn in 3½" (9 cm) on the lower edge, turning in ½" (13 mm) on the raw edge and press. Stitch close to the inner pressed edge.

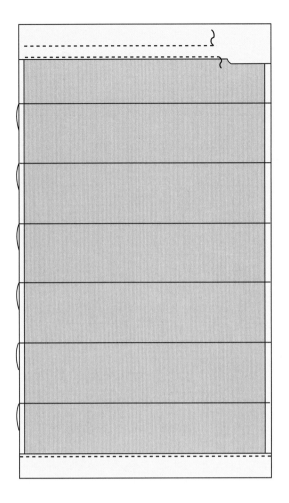

3 To make the tucks, bring the lines for each tuck together and stitch on the right side of the shade. Press all the tucks down.
Turn in 5½" (14 cm) on the upper edge, turning in ½" (13 mm) on the raw edge and press. Stitch close to the inner pressed edge.
To form the casing for the rod, stitch 1½" (3.8 cm) above the first stitching.

4 Insert the rod through the casing and place within the window frame at the desired height. Fold the tuck above the casing down, as shown.

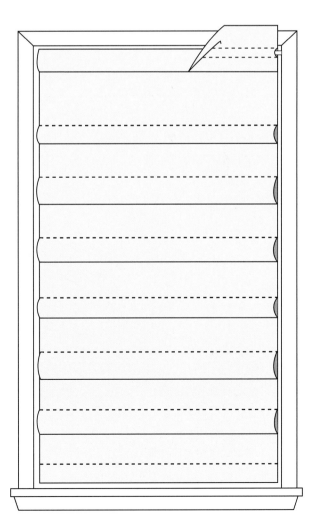

Origami Shade

$\mathcal{T}$he sculptural quality of this shade suits modern décor as beautifully as it would art deco décor. Its look is crisp and balanced. The shade moves up and down on cords threaded through rings positioned at the dowels for stability. The dowels also add an extra dimension of texture, showing through the sheer fabric.

materials list

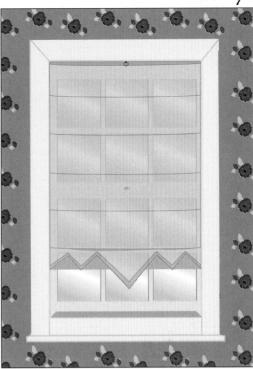

◆ **2 yds. fabric, 45" (115 cm) to 60" (152 cm) wide**

◆ **One tension rod the length of window width inside moldings**

◆ **Seven ½" (13 mm) diameter dowels (to fit inside window molding)**

◆ **Sixteen ½" (13 mm) plastic rings**

◆ **7⅞ yds. (6.8 m) ⅛" (3 mm) nylon cord**

◆ **Two screw eyes**

◆ **One awning cleat**

Window up to 42" (107 cm) wide and 60" (152 cm) long.

Fabric Suggestions: A light or medium weight, semi-sheer fabric, such as handkerchief linen, organza, cotton voile or tissue silk work best.

cutting instructions

1 Cut one section of fabric the width of the window, measured inside the moldings, plus 3" (7.5 cm) and 71" (180 cm) long.

▧ Right side of fabric

☐ Wrong side of fabric

2 To shape the lower edge of the shade, with right sides together, fold the shade in half lengthwise.
Measure 9½" (24 cm) up from the lower edge at outer corner, as shown; mark. Draw a line from the mark to the fold at the lower edge. Cut along the line.

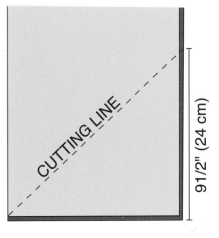

CUTTING LINE

91/2" (24 cm)

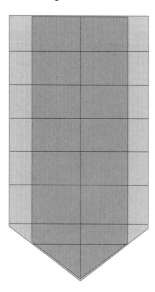

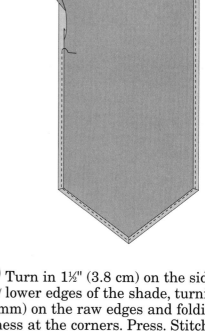

1 For a dowel placement template, rule a piece of paper the same length as the shade; starting at the top, first mark five lines 8¾" (22.2 cm) apart. Mark the next line 11¼" (28.5 cm) down. And then mark the last line 5½" (14 cm) down from the previous line. Lightly transfer the lines to the wrong side of the shade fabric.

2 Turn in 1½" (3.8 cm) on the side and lower edges of the shade, turning in ½" (13 mm) on the raw edges and folding in the fullness at the corners. Press. Stitch close to the inner pressed edges.

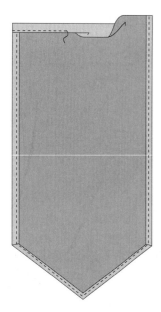

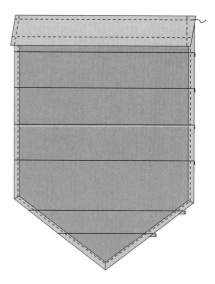

3 To form the casing for the tension rod, turn in 2" (5 cm) on the upper edge, turning in ½" (13 mm) on the raw edge and press. Stitch close to the inner pressed edge.

4 To form casings for the dowels, with wrong sides together, fold the shade along the transferred lines. Stitch ½" (13 mm) away from each of the folded edges.

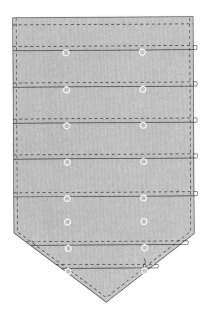

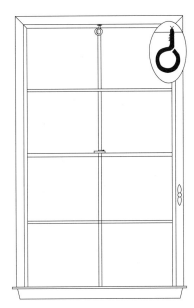

5 Insert the dowels into the casings, trimming to the correct length if necessary. Tack the rings to the right side of the shade at the dowel casings, 10" (26 cm) in from the sides, as shown, making sure that the rings are vertically aligned.

6 Install one screw eye to the center of the window frame and the remaining screw eye to the corner of the side you wish to install the awning cleat. Install the awning cleat at the desired location on the window frame.

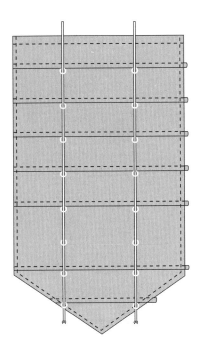

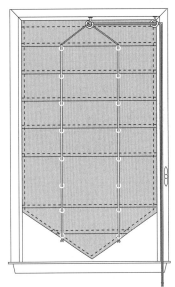

7 Cut the cord into two equal lengths. Tie one end of each cord to one of the bottom rings. Thread the cords up through the remaining rings.

8 Insert the tension rod through the upper casing and mount the shade in the window, behind the screw eyes, with the rings and cord facing you.
Thread the cords through the center screw eye, then the screw eye on the side. Knot the cords close to the last screw eye. This prevents the cord from tangling. Knot the ends of the cords together. Trim the ends evenly. Pull cords to raise and lower shades.

Window Drapery

These dramatic window dressings have a classic, timeless look. Any of these elegant designs suit every décor, be it traditional or contemporary. Made of sheer or semi-sheer fabrics, these drapes allow plenty of light in, and infuse the room with a warm glow.

Draped Scarves

The graceful folds of this treatment turn any window into a decorative showpiece. The design is enhanced here with bold borders and ornamental holdbacks. The asymmetrical panels can be adjusted to fit any window. This style is stunning.

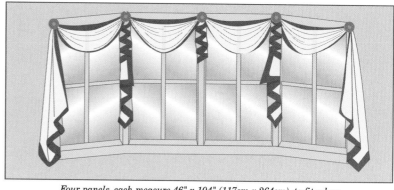

Four panels, each measure 46" x 104" (117cm x 264cm), to fit a bay window, 117" (297cm) wide.

materials list

Fabric Suggestions: Soft, sheer or semi-sheer fabrics, such as organdy, batiste or voile are the best for the center sections. Fabrics such as linen, cotton broadcloth, silk dupioni or damask are recommended for the borders.

Please note, both sides of the fabric and contrast fabric will show.

◆ **11 yds. (10.1 m) fabric, 45" (115 cm) wide**

◆ **8¼ yds. (7.32 m) contrast fabric, 45" (115 cm) wide**

◆ **Five decorative curtain hold-backs**

cutting instructions

1 For the center sections, cut four panels of fabric, each 40"(102cm) long and 98" (249 cm) long.

2 For the longer bands, cut eight sections of contrast fabric, each 8" (20.5 cm) wide and 98" (249 cm) long.

3 For the shorter bands, cut eight sections of contrast fabric, each 8" (20.5 cm) wide and 47" (120 cm) long.

tips

Take a tip from professional decorators, and take a small pouch with you on all shopping excursions. Include in the pouch dimensions of rooms, all window measurements, paint and fabric swatches, even polaroids of certain rooms. Leave it in your car or bag so you won't forget it. Then you'll always have the important information with you when you see that perfect bolt of fabric or decorative rod on sale!

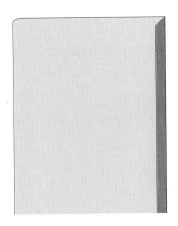

1 Turn in ½" (13 mm) on one long edge of each band section; press.

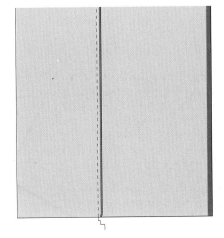

2 Pin the right side of the longer bands to the wrong side of the panels, having the raw edges even. Stitch the bands to the panels. Press the seam allowances toward the bands.

3 Turn the bands down, placing the pressed edges over the seams. Press the bands, creating a crease on the outer edge. Edgestitch the pressed inner edges of the bands in place. Baste the raw edges at the ends together.

4 Pin the right sides of the shorter bands to the wrong side of unfinished edges of the panels, having the long raw edges even. The ends should extend ½" (13 mm), as shown. Stitch the end bands to the panels. Press the seam allowances toward the bands.

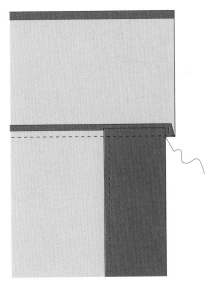

5 Turn in ½"(13mm) on the ends of the bands and press.

6 Fold the bands down, placing the pressed edges over the seams and press. Edgestitch the pressed inner edges of the bands in place. Slipstitch the ends of the bands together.

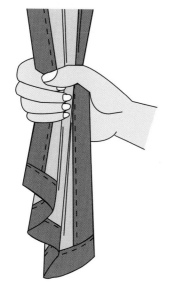

7 Fold each of the panels or scarves into three folds and pin mark.

8 Working from the center windows out, drape the scarves over the holdbacks, allowing a drop of approximately 8" (20.5 cm) at the center of each window. Adjust the draping of the scarves to your liking.

Fold Over Scarf

This window dressing's gentle cascades of fabric are a lovely way to decorate a single window, as seen here. They also look great on a pair of windows, especially flanking a fireplace or sofa. The panel can be draped over the holdback or released for privacy. Seen here, the Fold Over Scarf is quite elegant and demure. But bordered in a lively color, or with fanciful holdbacks, this same design can be quite charming.

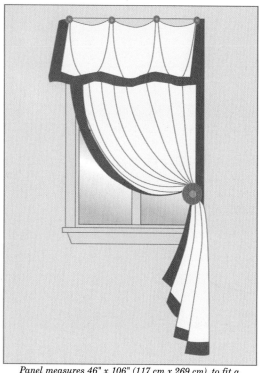

Panel measures 46" x 106" (117 cm x 269 cm), to fit a 34"(86.5cm) to 37"(94 cm) wide window.

materials list

Fabric Suggestions: Soft sheer or semi-sheer fabrics, such as cotton batiste, voile or organdy work best for the center of the panel. Linen, cotton broadcloth, silk dupioni, damask or satin are nice choices for the borders.

Please note, both sides of the fabric and contrast fabric will show.

◆ **2⅞ yds. (2.63 m) fabric, 45" (115 cm) wide**

◆ **2⅞ yds. (2.63 m) contrast fabric, 45" (115 cm) wide**

◆ **Four decorative drapery push pins**

◆ **One decorative hold-back**

cutting instructions

1 For the center panel, cut one section of fabric 40" (102 cm) wide and 100" (254 cm) long.

2 For the longer bands, cut two sections of contrast fabric, each 8" (20.5 cm) wide and 100" (254 cm) long.

3 For the shorter bands, cut two sections of contrast fabric, each 8" (20.5 cm) wide and 47" (120 cm) long.

Divide and mark width of window frame into three equal sections.

Install the hold back at the desired position on the window frame.

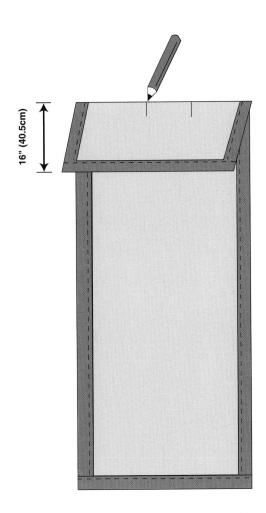

16" (40.5cm)

1 * To apply the bands, please refer to the instructions and illustrations on pages 79 and 80.

Turn down 16" (40.5 cm) on the upper edge of the panel to the outside and press it lightly, to create a soft crease. Divide and mark the pressed edge into three equal sections, excluding the bands.

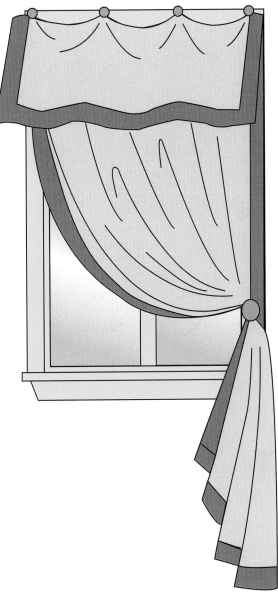

2 Match the markings on the creased edge of the panel to the markings on the window frame. Using your decorative drapery push pins, secure the panel to the frame, as shown. Drape the panel over the holdback, as you desire.

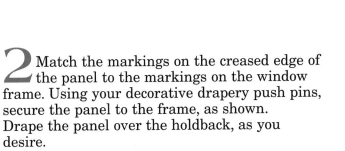

Double Scarf

his sprightly treatment is a wonderful way to top off any window that needs a light touch. Like a valance, this design needs no drapes, being an open and sunny decoration. As pictured here, accented with gold trim and holdbacks, the Double Scarf appears classic and formal. Yet it works equally well in an informal setting, made of gingham and cotton cord.

materials list

Please note, both sides of the fabrics will show.

◆ 2⅞ yds. (2.63 m) fabric, 45" (115 cm) wide

◆ 2⅞ yds. (2.63 m) fabric, 45" (115 cm) wide

◆ **Two decorative drapery holdbacks**

◆ **One 32" cord with tassels**

Fabric Suggestions: Soft, sheer or semi-sheer fabrics, such as cotton batiste, voile or organdy are great for the center panel. Linen, cotton broadcloth, taffeta or satin are good choices for the borders.

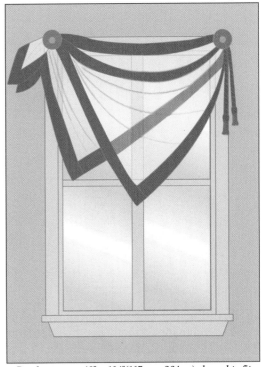

Panel measures 46" x 104"(117cm x 264cm), draped to fit window 34"(86.5cm) to 37"(94cm) wide.

cutting instructions

1 For the center panel, cut one section of fabric 40" (102 cm) wide and 98" (249 cm) long.

3 For the shorter bands, cut two sections of contrast fabric, each 8" (20.5 cm) wide and 48" (122 cm) long.

2 For the longer bands, cut two sections of contrast fabric, each 8"(20.5cm) wide and 98"(249cm) long.

tips

If you do not find drapery holdbacks to your liking, a great alternative is to use door knobs. Good sources for antique doorknobs of glass, crystal, brass or porcelain are salvage yards, flea markets, yard sales and, of course, antique stores. You can also create unique tiebacks by using silk scarves, cord or braided fabric.

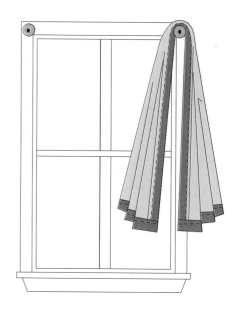

1 To apply the bands, please refer to the instructions and illustrations on pages 79 and 80, steps 1 - 6. Fold the panel lengthwise into three or four folds.

2 Drape the center of the panel over the right holdback, as shown.

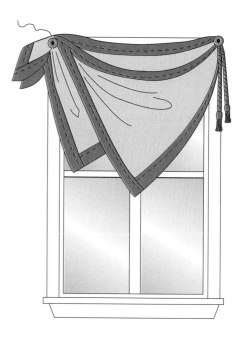

3 Drape the inner corner of the right half of the panel over the left holdback.

4 Drape the outer corner of the remaining half of the panel over the left holdback, as shown. Adjust the draping as you desire. Tack the corners of the scarf in place at the holdback, if necessary. Drape the cord with tassels around the right holdback and tack to secure in place.

Handkerchief Panel

The Handkerchief Panel is dramatic and different, but still quite easy to make. This treatment shows the magic you can achieve with the deft use of cord and tassel to drape a single panel. Although this treatment is stationary, the sheer fabric allows plenty of light in, creating a warm glow.

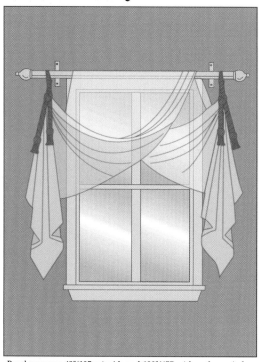

*Panel measures 42"(107cm) wide and 188"(477cm) long, for a window
up to 42"(107cm) wide , that is approximately 60"(152cm) long.*

materials list

**Fabric Suggestions: Sheer
fabrics, such as voile,
batiste or organdy with or
without tone-on-tone
printing or textured
weave work very well in
this treatment.**

**Please note, both sides of
the fabric will show.**

◆ **5¼ yds. (4.77 m) fabric,
45" (155 cm) wide**

◆ **Two cords with tassels
(the cord should be at
least 32" (81 cm) long)**

◆ **1½" (3.8 cm) to 2" (5 cm)
diameter decorative rod**

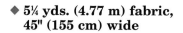

cutting instructions

1 Trim the selvages from the long edges
of the fabric.

2 Trim the ends of the fabric so that they
are straight, removing as little fabric as
possible.

3 Install your rod on the wall above the
window, following the manufacturer's
instructions.

tips

This panel is shown with a plain edge, but also
looks lovely with a trim around the edges—a
fold over braid or fringe, perhaps. A trim
enhances the visual effect of the draping. To
trim the entire outer edge of the panel, you
would need 13 1/2 yds. (12.4 m) of trim.

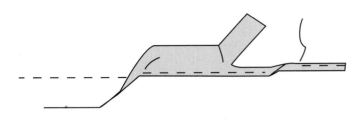

1 Stitch ½" (13 mm) from the trimmed long edges of the panel. Turn in and press the edges along the stitching.

Trim the raw edges very close to the stitching.

Turn the edges in again, encasing the raw edges. Stitch the inner edge in place, as shown.

2 Make a narrow hem at the ends of the panel.

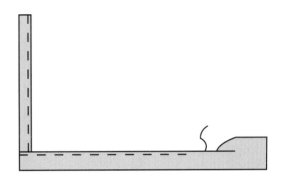

20" (51cm)   20" (51cm)

3 Hang your panel over the rod, making sure that the lower edges are even. Measure up 20" (51 cm) from the lower edge. Pin mark the measurements.

4 Hang the corded tassels over the ends of the rod. Holding each end of the panel at the pinmark, tack to each cord as shown in the illustration. Adjust the position of the panel if necessary.

Grecian Swag and Drape

This stunning window dressing is reminiscent of the fashions of the Ancient Greeks. Its grace and sophistication would suit any formal living or dining room. The treatment is actually two pieces; the left panel is draped over the rod. The right panel is draped over the rod then swagged to the left and tacked to the rod.

materials list

♦ 11¼ yds. (10.3 m) fabric, 45" (115cm) wide

♦ 1" (2.5 cm) to 2" (5 cm) diameter decorative rod with brackets

♦ Staple gun or tacks and hammer

Fabric Suggestions: The lightest sheers and tone on tone sheers in pale colors or whites work best. Cotton gauze, cotton voile and batiste, handkerchief linen and crepe de chine are all very good for this window treatment.

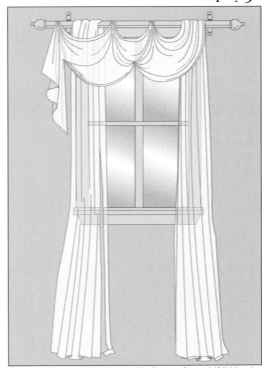

Window up to 42"(107cm) wide. Drapes hang 90"(229cm) from floor and puddle approximately 5"(12.5cm) to 6"(15cm) onto the floor.

cutting instructions

1 Cut the fabric into two panels; one panel 193" (490 cm) long and one panel 207" (526 cm) long.

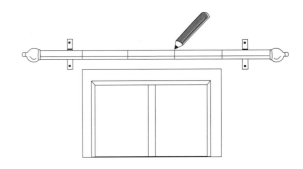

2 Cut the fabric into two panels; one panel 193" (490 cm) long and one panel 207" (526 cm) long.

Trim ½" (13 mm) from the selvages on both sides of each panel.

Trim the ends straight, trimming as little fabric as possible.

Install your decorative rod in the desired position above the window, following manufacturer's instructions.

Divide the length of the rod between the outside of the window moldings into three sections. Lightly mark the pole.

tips

This style looks exceptional, using more exotic and unusual fabrics, such as sari silks, light weight Balinese batik silks or embellished organdy.

1 Stitch ½" (13 mm) from the trimmed edges of the panels. Turn in the edges along the stitching and press. Trim the raw edges very close to the stitching. Turn in the edges again, encasing the raw edges. Stitch the inner edges in place, as shown.

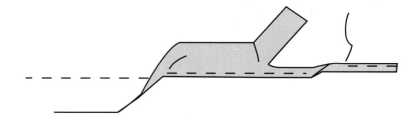

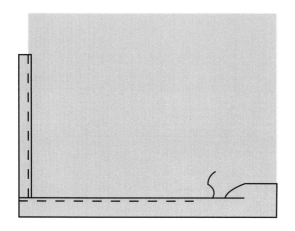

2 Make narrow hems at the ends of the panels.

3 Hang the shorter panel over the left side of the rod, puddling the ends evenly on the floor.

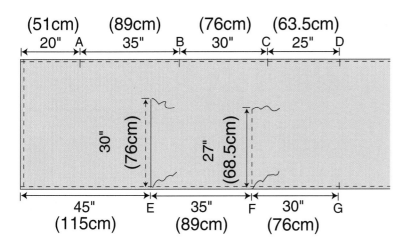

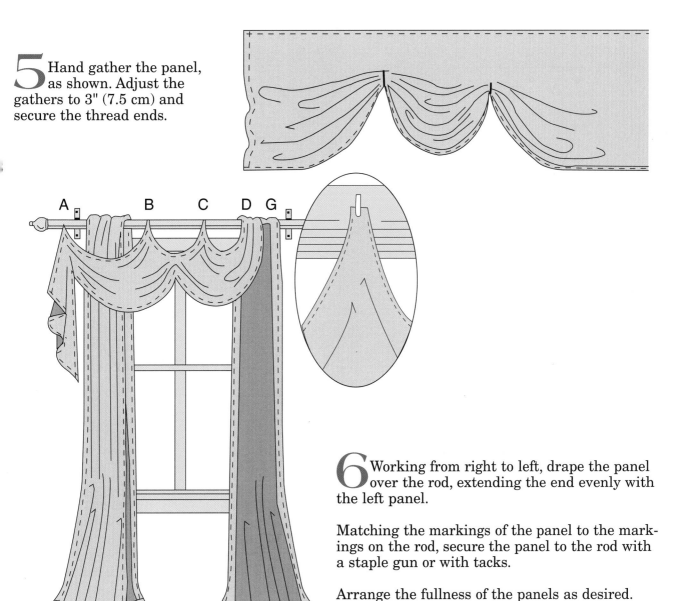

4 Working on a flat surface, mark the remaining panel following this diagram.
Measure up 30" (76 cm) from point E and 27" (68.5 cm) from point F. Lightly mark these measurements.

5 Hand gather the panel, as shown. Adjust the gathers to 3" (7.5 cm) and secure the thread ends.

6 Working from right to left, drape the panel over the rod, extending the end evenly with the left panel.

Matching the markings of the panel to the markings on the rod, secure the panel to the rod with a staple gun or with tacks.

Arrange the fullness of the panels as desired.

Templates

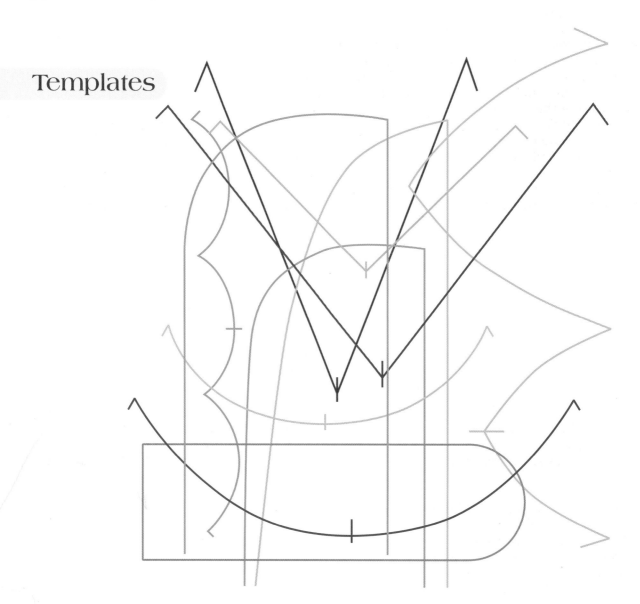

All the templates pictured here need to be enlarged at 286% for the projects in this book. If you do not have access to a photocopy machine, most copy shops will do this for a small fee.

Once you have enlarged the template shape, you need to transfer the shape to thin cardboard, oak tag or Bristol board. One method is to glue the photocopied enlarged shape to the cardboard and cut the shape out. Another method is to trace the shape onto the cardboard and then cut it out. This sturdy template can be traced many times without the edges becoming distorted.

Place the lower edge of the template on the lower edge of the fabric, matching the center of the template and the fabric. It is best to work from the center, out to either side. Trace the shape onto the fabric. Cut the fabric along the traced line(s).

Bias is used when we want a fabric to drape particularly well or to mold well around curves and corners as for binding and piping.

To make your own bias binding first calculate the width of the bias strip. To do so, add three measurements together:
• two times your binding width
• ⅛" (3 mm) to ¼" (6 mm) for the thickness of the edge you are binding

• two times your seam allowance.

For example, if you want a 1" (25 mm) binding and you have ½" (13 mm) seam allowances, you need to cut your strips 3⅛" (7.9 cm) to 3¼" (8.2 cm) wide.

To make your own piping, the width of the bais strip is determined by adding two measurements:
• the circumference of the piping cord

Bias

• two times the seam allowance. For example, if you have piping cord 1" (25 mm) in diameter and ½" (13 mm) seam allowance, you need to cut your strips 2" (5 cm) wide.

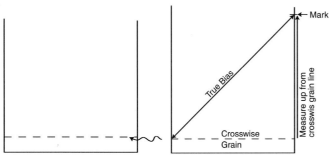

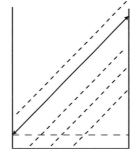

1 The first step in cutting bias strips is to determine true bias. True bias is 45° from the lengthwise and crosswise grain.

To find true bias first establish the crosswise grain. The best way to find the crosswise grain is to pull a thread. Make a small incision in the selvage, as shown. Next, carefully pull out one of the crosswise threads. The space left by the thread indicates the crosswise grain.

Measure the width of the fabric along the crosswise grain.
Measure that same distance up from the crosswise grain line along the selvage; mark. Draw a line from the mark, down diagonally to the far selvage at the crosswise grain line. This is true bias.

2 Measuring from the true bias line, draw your strips. Using scissors or a rotary cutter and self healing mat, cut out the strips along the lines.

3 To piece the strips together, pin them right sides together, as in the diagram. Stitch, as shown. Piece enough strips together to bind or pipe the desired area, adding a little extra for samples and possible experimentation.

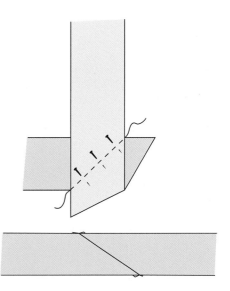

Index